18 Golfing Secrets

STRATEGIES, TIPS, DRILLS
AND PHILOSOPHIES TO SHOOT
LOWER SCORES

Chris Baker

Dedicated to my parents David & Anne Baker.

Thank you for always pausing in your tracks and taking the time to give me your undivided time and attention. I love you indefinitely and owe you everything.

Christopher:
"Define Success?"

Elsa:
"Being in your power"

Christopher:
"What is Power?"

Elsa:
"Truth".

Elsa Valentine

"Well we're waiting."
Judge Smails, Caddyshack

THE LESSONS

I'm always 'working.' It looks like work to them, but it feels like play to me.
—NAVAL RAVIKANT

MY STORY AND HOW THIS BOOK CAME TO BE

It's unbelievable how much you don't know about the game you've been playing all your life.
—**MICKEY MANTLE**

Become who you are by learning who you are.
—**PINDAR**

I first got into golf at the age of 12. Since that first well-struck shot, it has been a quest for unattainable perfection.

Around six feet of shelf space in my home is occupied by spines of leather journals. I have recorded nearly every single round of golf.

Keeping this compendium of recipes has helped me identify what I was working on when I was playing my best: the principles, philosophies, tips, lessons, and ideas. More importantly, the drills, habits, and routines I was implementing when I was playing my worst.

Some people would call this OCD, I just always viewed it as a collection of my experiences with golf on paper.

My dream was always to play on the European Tour. Although I fell short of this dream, I have been fortunate enough to have some small wins along the way. These include:

- First golfing handicap 13 aged 12
- First broke par at the age of 13
- Won my 1st Men's Clubs Championship aged 15

- One of six to represent GB&I against America on the Swifts Tour, winning 20/21 matches. The team was made up of the likes of Nick Faldo and Ronan Raffety's sons, also Matt Wallace (European/ PGA Tour)
- Three Men's Club Champion at three different clubs
- Winner of the regional Faldo Series
- Winner of the Halford Hewitt 2010, the biggest amateur team tournament in the world
- Gained a golfing scholarship to the Queens University of Charlotte, North Carolina
- Winner of two NCAA Carolina Conference Championship rings
- Caddy on the European Tour Qualifying School in Spain 2015-2018

But, also playing this game, I have:
- Recreated the Tin Cup Scene when Roy McAvoy snapped all of his clubs, having finished last in a tournament by five strokes and then listed the remaining unbroken ones on ebay.
- Faked an injury during a 36 holes county event, because I was playing so bad and wanted to avoid my handicap going up.
- Fell completely out of love with the game. I went traveling around the world and did not pick up my clubs for 18 months
- Suffered from the yips off the tee and around the green for two years
- My handicap quadrupled going from +1 to 2 in a matter of two seasons and I failed to break 80 the majority of the time

- Invested so much time into this game, with no pay off, making me feel uncommitted to other areas of life. This created a mind set of "what if it doesn't work, and I have poured many hours into this and got nothing out of it"

Although it has been tough, it is a game that I have obsessed over and feel lucky to play.

I never turned pro. I was never good enough, not even close. As an amateur, I have been fortunate enough for the game to take me around the world. From Europe, South Africa, America, Australia, to even some remote islands in the Indian Ocean. I have met inspirational coaches, battled till the 18th hole with strangers and met many of my closest friends, all from the game of golf.

For the last three years, I have also been a podcast host on the show, "Making A Club Champion", a series of actionable interviews featuring some of the best golf coaches from around the world.

I have met the likes of pressure and performance coach Dave Alred, to Francesco Molinari and Luke Donald. I have interviewed putting coach Phill Kenyon, to the likes of Rory Mcilroy, Hendrik Stenson, Justin Rose, Lee Westwood, Louis Oosthuizen, and Martin Kaymer. Pia Nilsson and Lynn Marriott, founders of Vision 54. Who have helped nine different major winners and four players claim the elusive world number one ranking.

This book will cover a range of ideas, which will include the following:

- How to implement specific actionable drills that some of the best coaches in the world share with their students
- How to navigate your ball around the course more effectively

- How not to waste time drilling in bad habits on the range
- How to hit more fairways, find more greens, and hole more putts
- How to develop a winning mindset and mental strength
- How to use nutrition for performance and keep your energy levels high during your round
- How to improve your relationship with the game using a stoic philosophy and mindfulness

And much more.

Over the last 18+ years of playing this game, learning from the best coaches around the world, there have been a handful of methods that I have found to work and stand the test of time.

Although I do not have the answers to solving golf, these are the 18 lessons that have worked best for me.

I have longed to distill these insights into an ultimate set of concise "cliff notes," that I can revisit when lost and in need of direction.

I first started to culminate these notes in 2013. Seven years later, digging and sourcing through the archives, **these are the strategies, tips, drills and philosophies to shoot lower scores**.

I hope you enjoy reading them as much as I have enjoyed writing them.

To your greatness, both on and off the fairways.

Kia kaha,
Chris
Colonna & Small's Cafe, Bath, 2017

SETTING THE EXPECTATIONS EARLY AND HOW TO USE THIS BOOK

If information was the answer, we would all be billionaires with perfect abs.
—DEREK SIVERS

The more certain you appear about something, the less you know about it. The sign of the true expert is his modest awareness of how much more there is to know; how complex and nuanced the subject at hand insists on remaining.
—DERREN BROWN, HAPPY

My role is to give options, not to give an answer.
—MARK BULL

With any cookbook, you are not going to like all the recipes. There may be one or two, however, which you are going to drool over, tell the world about, and cook for the next 20+ years. Some you will try, others you will never venture to attempt again.

But the most important thing is that you tried and tested it yourself. Through continuous attempts and a process of testing, measuring, learning, and failing, out will discover what you like and what does not work for you and your game.

My goal for this book is to make you the most effective and authentic golfer you can be.

If one great lesson comes from this book that you install in your game and you become marginally better - to me that is a win.

Most of these lessons I continually work on myself. I forget to do the small things that work well. I stop practicing them, I get lazy, take them for granted, and ultimately, my game suffers.

The game ebbs and flows like life. There are always things to be working through and practicing .

I hope that if this book has found its way into your hands, the lessons will inspire and help your game too.

How to Use This Book:

The way of success is the way of continuous pursuit of knowledge.
—NAPOLEON HILL

When you are not practicing, remember, someone, somewhere is practicing, and when you meet him, he will win.
—BILL BRADLEY

1. If you sit down and read this in one sitting, I cannot stop you. It is a short book and should hopefully be a fun and light read. My only request is that you come back to it and read it again, but not in one sitting. The pages in this book are to be thought about and tested, and not rushed. Some pages may resonate with you straight away, some when read years later; some you may find contradict one another and make no sense.

    If you have played this game for a good number of years, you know by now there is no quick fix. I intended to write this as a book for you to test and explore with your game, perhaps journal on a page that strikes you, put a line through a page that doesn't, mark a page that you want to revisit.

As Mark Bull (Biomechanics coach to some of the world's very best golfers) once told me, "we are all inherently different, the way you walk is different from the way I walk. There is no one protocol that will work for everyone." You are so unique and so different. It concerns me when I hear people say. "You must do this.", or, "You must do that." The reality: You shouldn't do anything that doesn't work for you.

Treat these chapters as a mini set of experiments and hypotheses. Implement, gather feedback, then drop it or keep it. If something doesn't grab you right now, move on. If you are peppering the flags with your wedges but you cannot find the planet off the tee, read lessons on the long game and come back to the short game another time. Find the lessons which are going to be most impactful for you and your game now; take action, and let the others wait. Make the ideas in this book your ideas.

2. If you are expecting instant results and/or looking for another golf magazine headline: *"Guaranteed extra 30 yards and 3 shots off your game"*, let me save you time now. Drop this book and continue to seek instant gratification. This book is about playing the long game. These lessons will take hard, conscious, diligent work to genuinely change. You can't change a person unless they want to make a change. Be patient and play the long game with your development.

3. This is also not a technical book. So, if something sticks with you, take the idea, drill, or philosophy and talk it over with your coach. Some lessons will have actionable takeaways to work on.

4. Be sceptical. These are lessons that have worked for me and my game. Please keep that in mind whilst reading. But do not use

scepticism as an excuse for inaction. Take action. Be proactively sceptical, not defensively sceptical.

5. If you aren't curious about it, you'll never be good at it. I don't care about why you pick up your clubs, I am more worried about why you put them down. If my book takes you to win majors, gaining your card on the European/PGA Tour, to winning your club championship or your Saturday medal; if it takes you to walking down the fairway of your home club one summer's afternoon surrounded by your grandchildren, with not a care in the world, stripping it down the middle time and time again - to me, these are all wins.

FINAL WORDS...

Inside the front cover of my first golfing journal aged 12, I neatly wrote the following words by Walter Hagen:

"Don't forget to smell the roses along the way."

Eighteen years later, I still think about this quote.

For all you seek, it is too easy to want more and increase the speed and size of your life, but if you're not content with what you have, you'll never be content with what you add.

I hope you find what you are looking for.

Now make yourself a good cup of coffee, and let's begin.

There is a lot to learn and unlearn.

To all your greatness,
Chris,
Philz Coffee, San Francisco, 2014

LESSON NO. 1:

HOW TO CALCULATE YARDAGES LIKE A TOUR CADDY

My first caddy gig was at Claremont Country Club in Oakland, California.

With views overlooking the Golden Gate Bridge, if you wanted to join this fine establishment, it would set you back a cool $100k plus subs each year.

Being exclusively for private and members-only, it was more than a golf course. Families would turn up in their big SUVs, mums would go off for tennis lessons, kids would spend the day at the pool, and the guys would play golf. They would all reunite on the terrace in the afternoon, have dinner, cocktails and mingle with friends, watching the California sun drop over the mountains.

Each morning I would walk to the club and wait in the caddy shack.

Everything about this place was pristine, except for the caddy shack.

A small hut tucked hidden behind the pro shop was what we called "home". The inside looked like it hadn't had a lick of paint for about 50 years. The floor was filled with fag ends, peanut shells, tees, and ripped scorecards to make rollies from.

About eight to ten guys would be rammed in the caddy shack. We would be sitting, dressed in our white overalls like the caddies at The

Masters, waiting for our names to be called out from the head pro to get a loop for the day. These guys were lifers, they came from all over the world and could tell intoxicating stories until the sun came down.

Some days, I would wait all day with anticipation for my name to be called out. Unfortunately, due to the nature of the position there was never any guarantee of a call up, and such days would slip by without purpose. Time was filled with poker, card games, reading a book, or listening to a podcast. For a one bag loop (18 holes), you would get 40 bucks, plus tip. On invitational days or competition days, you could earn good money. All the caddies looked forward to the invitational days. Members' guests were often very generous when it came to the tips. These were our majors. These were our pay days.

Waiting all day in that caddy shack taught my 24-year-old self the art of patience. Some days felt like the scene from the Gladiator, all waiting in the dungeons before heading out into the colosseum to help entertain the rich and famous.

My first caddy lesson was from the head pro of that golf club: "show up, stay up, and shut up". It was a quick lesson.

Getting your first gig was the hardest. One caddy had been working there 50+ years. He could barely walk. His skin was burnt to a crisp and he would still march into the sun carrying the members clubs. You got a loop if one of the regular caddies failed to show up. You were built on reputation and relied on being liked by the members. Getting on with the head pro was also very important. I never liked the idea of sucking up to anyone, but he called the shots and it helped if he liked you. Some guys in the caddy shack never got called out.

After getting my first few loops, I started to think of ways in which I could build my regulars. I would try to offer more value than the other caddies by doing the player's stats for their rounds.

In anticipation of being called out for a loop, I had devised my own card that would enable me to accurately document my clients' statistics. During the round, I would write down specific stats on their game, how many fairways and greens they had hit, the number of putts they had taken, percentage in up and downs, etc. Some players liked it. I also learned that most players hated it. Most of them looked at me as if to say, "why did you do that"? In hindsight, I probably should have asked them before the round started. Lesson learnt.

I think a lot of them didn't want to know that they had missed every fairway, hit only a couple of greens, taken 40 puts, and shot 15 over their handicap. There were a lot of big characters at the club. Most of the members were highly successful in their careers, which instilled a fiercely competitive ego that would often transfer onto the course.

They were extraordinarily competitive with one another. Most of the time they played money matches, with enormous amounts of cash being exchanged in the car park. The value prop started to work and the golfers who took interest in their performance became my regulars. I had done just a little bit more than what was asked for, and they appreciated that and wanted to learn more about their game.

Some players would talk, some would not. Some would let you hit shots, some would tip handsomely, some would shaft you, some wanted precise yardages, some wanted just a club. It would be a long day if you and your player do not get on or see eye to eye. You had to quickly learn what sort of player you had for the day by getting to know their mannerisms in the first couple of holes. The great caddies were like hawks, they had this hyper awareness of how to bring out the very best from their player. It was like a different performing act with each new player. It was a real skill.

If a player had a rangefinder, I would use that to give them a number. Most of the time we would take yardages off the sprinkler heads in the fairway. If the pin position was front, middle or back, we would just take off a few here or there. Some caddies didn't even need to look at the sprinkler heads, they knew the course so well they would just tell you what the yardage was. I often cross-referenced their numbers if my player had a Bushnell. They were incredibly accurate.

I definitely asked way too many questions. As I knew this was just going to be a small phase in my life, I thought I may as well take advantage of the opportunity while I had it.

I wanted to know what these guys did for a living, how they lived these dreamy American lives, what their story was, where they lived, what life advice they had to offer. From the outside in, they looked like very happy people and seemed to have life about right. I wanted to know their secrets.

At the time, I lived a very strange and surreal life. I was dating a very successful and attractive high-tech businesswoman. She was 42 and I lived with her in a mid-century modern home that looked like something out of a James Bond movie, overlooking the golf course and the view of San Francisco. If you have ever watched "The Pursuit of Happiness", I lived behind that big white house, which Will Smith goes to before the ball game with his son. It was stunning.

I was earning $90 - $120 on a good day, then retreating to my girlfriend's multi-million dollar house in the hills. None of it made sense. I never told anyone at the club; it was my private life. The money earned from one to two loops a day would disappear into dust. We would venture into the city of San Francisco most nights, go out for drinks, or try the best tasting menus the city had to offer. On the weekends we would go to Napa Valley or fly to Hawaii for a couple of days, staying at the finest five-star hotel, the St Regis in Kauai being our frequent stop of choice. The money I earned paid for the tips at most of these places. I was out of my league.

On Mondays, caddies could play the course for free. I would get to the club when the sun was just coming up and leave the course when the sun was going down. It reminded me of my junior days where I would spend my summers at the club. I would fill up on nuts from the halfway house to save money and not buy lunch. It was a great hack to be able to play golf for free at a spectacular private club.

I worked two seasons at the country club. I was supposed to get married to the beautiful millionaire, but just couldn't go through with it. I left the country and headed back home to the UK – a story for another time.

It was four years later when I got back into caddying again. A friend who I competed against at college in America had taken his game to the next level and was really going for it. I saw a post on Facebook saying he was off to try and earn his tour card on the European Tour. I reached out to him and asked if he wanted a caddy for the week. I told him, "no payment needed, but if you want someone on the bag, I would love to help out."

He sent me a message back instantly and took me up on my offer. Days later we were walking the course in Spain mapping out our plan for the week. I found myself caddying at one of the most anticipated and dreaded events any tour player will experience.

The European Tour Qualifying School in Spain is made up of six brutal rounds and if you finish in the top 24 spots, you earn your tour card. See it as the final stage of interviews for your dream job, competing against a pack of hungry wolves all wanting their shot in the limelight too.

Unless you have some wealthy backers, most of these players are working part-time jobs to make ends meet while pursuing their dream. It ain't all sunshine and rainbows. With entrance fees, hotel costs, food, and flights, it is an expensive game if you are not making cuts and finishing high up on the leader board week in, week out. As such, many great players never make it due to lack of financial resources.

Very few words are exchanged between players, as throughout the week they all become immersed in themselves and their game. The qualifying school is not a fun place to be. It is a place to show up, get the job done and move on. You can feel the pressure and tension among the players at these events. They all want to be competing on the world stage at the biggest of competitions where all the fame, money and attention is.

Walking on the range, I saw Alvaro Quiros, Gonzalo Fernández-Castaño, also the major winner who stopped Tiger in his tracks - Y. E Yang. Just a few years ago, these guys were winning tour events, majors, and millions of dollars and now they are scrambling to earn a living. How the mighty fall and what a brutally honest game.

At breakfast one morning, Eddie Pepperell was sitting across from me eating by himself and wearing headphones. Just weeks prior, he needed a par down the last at the Portugal Masters, but he snapped-hooked his tee shot resulting in a double bogey and losing his card. He was now fighting for his future. He looked to be filled with worry and fear. If I could define a lonely experience, this looked to be it.

This whole time, these were the only emotions that emerged for me; mentally I was never built tough enough to compete and play this game for a living. I was nervous carrying the bag, let alone having to compete.

As a caddy, you must always think and be one step ahead of your player. On the range, the first thing you do is check the distances of every yardage marker. I would draw out the entire range each morning on the back of our yardage book. With pictures of 50, 100, 150, 200, and 250-yard markers. The 50-yard markers were coming out at 53, 100 - 104, 150 - 155. It was this intense level of detail about every-thing which I started to pick upon. These guys left no stone unturned.

Clubs came back to you quickly. You needed them cleaned to perfection, a single hint of mud in the grooves was not an option. This could result in a flyer and a shot dropped. On the course, you have to establish strict routines. Some players like to drink and eat on certain holes. I remember always giving my player food on holes 4, 8, 12 and would hand him his water bottle after most tee shots. My school mot-to in America was, "non ministrari sed ministrare". Not to be served but to serve. This perfectly summed up the role of a caddy: to serve your player in their best way possible.

Practice rounds consist of creating a game plan for the week – places to hit it off the tee to give your best angles into the pin positions and easy uphill putts. It was all worked backward from the uphill putt. (Review lesson no. 9 for more on this)

When I first started out caddying, I had no idea how to calculate yardages. Having grown up playing golf with a rangefinder, it was all calculated in a matter of seconds. Bushnell the flag, take off a few here and hit the number. But with no Bushnell's allowed on the tour, it had to be done the "old school" way.

Despite getting the caddy job, I had to swallow my pride and inform the player that I had no idea how to do the job I was there to do. One afternoon in Spain, my player sat me down and taught me all about yardages and the system he used to get the right number to the relative club.

Remember, much of this game is about doing the things you are in control of well. You can't control the ball once it's left the club, but you are in control of the process beforehand.

So, understanding how to do your yardages like a tour caddy will give you every best opportunity to hit the ball in the landing zones you need to find.

Here are the tour caddy secrets I learned that afternoon.

1. Find the number

When working out what yardage it is to the pin, the first thing is to find the total overall number to the flag. From there we can crunch our numbers on what we want to do next.

So, whether you are using a Bushnell or some other device, this is where it all starts.

- For this example, we have just hit a great tee shot down the middle of a par 4, we have lasered the flag, and we have 150 yards left to the hole.

2. Look at the Lie

The lie dictates everything. If it is below or above your feet, this will indicate whether you are going to be hitting a draw or fade.

If the ball has finished on an uphill lie, it is going to add some loft to your club. The ball will also spin more and then come up short. If the ball has finished on a downhill lie, it is going to decrease, and the ball will come out a little lower and faster off the club face. You will need to add or subtract a few yards based on the lie of the ball.

- The ball has finished on an uphill section of the fairway. For this, we will add an arbitrary number of say +3 yards to compensate for the ball potentially spinning a little more than normal. 150 + 3 yards. The new number to the flag = 153 yards.

3. Putting a Number on the Wind

The next thing to check for is the wind. Like Tiger Woods coming down the stretch at The Masters, the best thing to do is toss some grass into the air, check the direction it is coming from and then put a number on it.

You will start to get a feel for how many yards a light, medium or strong wind is. Once again, plus or minus if it is helping or into.

- For this shot, we have tossed up our grass, and the wind is moving quite strongly into. We put a number on the wind of +5. New Number 153 + 5 = 158 yards to the flag.

4. Landing Zone

If we can get the ball past the hole, we will leave ourselves on an up-hill putt. The greens are fairly soft and not rolling much either after the first bounce. We want to land the ball all the way to the hole and ideally let it finish past the pin. So, we add an additional +2 yards to make sure we get the ball to land hole high and then finish past the hole after it has rolled out.

- For this shot, the new number and final total number of landing the ball into the landing zone, with consideration of lie, wind and green is 158 + 2 = 160 yards

What once was a smooth eight iron is now a good seven. Calculating your yardages is a real skill and discipline and is the difference between gaining shots on the course and making unforced errors.

LESSON NO. 2:

HOW PLAYING UNDISCIPLINED GOLF IS CRUSHING YOUR GAME

One minute you're bleeding. The next minute you're hemorrhaging. The next minute you're painting the Mona Lisa.
—MAC O'GRADY

Take the piano teacher...he always says, Relax, relax. But how can you relax while your fingers are rushing over the keys? Yet they have to relax. The singing teacher and the golf pro say exactly the same thing. And in the realm of spiritual exercises we find that the person who teaches mental prayer does too. We have somehow to combine relaxation with activity... The personal conscious self being a kind of small island in the midst of an enormous area of consciousness... What has to be relaxed is the personal self, the self that tries too hard, that thinks it knows what is what, that uses language. This has to be relaxed in order that the multiple powers at work within the deeper and wider self may come through and function as they should. In all psychophysical skills we have this curious fact of the law of reversed effort: the harder we try, the worse we do the thing.
—ALDOUS HUXLEY

Golfers who play *impressive golf*:
- Attack drivable par 4s and take on most par 5's in two
- See the flag and only the flag, Hit every shot at the pin and take on aggressive lines

- Have the ability to make lots of birdies, but also the tendency to make lots of mistakes
- Hit impressive long drives and impressive memorable shots

They are the gambler, the risk-taker and lack patience. If they were a boxer, they would be looking for the knockout punch in the first round. In a match-play situation, these golfers are going to bury you 8&7, or you will do the same to them.

They define the phrase "hot and cold", flamboyant and loud.

No one likes fighting people who are unpredictable and have nothing to lose. Their form is temporary and relies heavily on timing, good breaks, and having confidence on the day. It is impressive golf that comes and goes.

If you could spot this person in a casino, they would be the one playing the large hands, going all-in or nothing. With this type of golfer, you come in after your round and talk about some spectacular shots that they pulled off: an epic long drive or a miraculous shot out of the rough, or a shot through a forest of trees that found the green.

Then there are the golfers who go out and play *unimpressive golf*. They:

- Play the percentages and plod their way around the golf course like a chess match
- Hit unimpressive shots that find the wide side of the fairways and wide side of the greens
- They hit away from the intended target most of the time
- If they find danger, they take their penalty get the ball back to a yardage in which they are strong and give themselves a putt for par

If they were playing poker, they would patiently wait until that perfect hand came along and only then would they bet big. If they were a boxer, they would take the time to study and analyze their opponent. If they were a batsman at the crease, they would wait for that perfect ball to come along.

With this type of golfer, you come in after your round and ask yourself, "how did they just shoot a 69! I hit it so much better than them."

This golfer quietly goes about their business. They are incognito. They are the ultimate embodiment of stealth.

Their form is consistent week on week. If you were to play with them, you might consider them unimpressive.

But the golfer who "scores well" on a consistent basis has learned how to play golf well.

Although we all would like to pull off those remarkable shots that are talked about in the clubhouse after the round, golf is not a game about ego and pulling off memorable shots. It is the art of being in control of your ball, being disciplined, staying patient for 18 holes, and letting the opportunities come to you.

LESSON NO. 3:

WHAT TO THINK WHEN OVER THE BALL

Every day that you don't practice is one day longer before you achieve greatness.

—BEN HOGAN

To think is easy. To act is hard. But the hardest thing in the world is to act in accordance with your thinking.

—JOHANN WOLFGANG

The music is the space between the notes. The music is not in the notes but in the silence between them.

—CLAUDE DEBUSSY

Same thoughts always lead to the same choices, same choices lead to the same behavior and the same behaviors lead to same experiences and the same experiences produce the same emotions and these emotions drive the very same thoughts.

—DR JOE DIZPENSA

Hard Choices, easy life, easy choices, hard life.

—JERZY GREGORY

Good thinking, good golf. Bad thinking, bad golf.

—MOE NORMAN

The Berkshire Trophy is one of the UK's great amateur trophies. With the likes of Nick Faldo, Gary Whisltholme, Ross Fisher, Eddie Pepperl as past winners, it is a privilege to play in and one of the toughest to win in the amateur circuit. If you make the cut, it is considered a great achievement for any amateur golfer.

I had waited nearly 10+ years to play in this event, yet I was standing over the first tee shot, not being able to pull the club back. I was stuck with what to do.

Looking down the 1st fairway, I hit a moment of overwhelming complexity. After my name was announced, I pulled a club out of the bag and made a few practice swings. The club felt so alien in my hands. I questioned what grip I was supposed to be using. I could not see a target, and I had no idea of my swing. I was completely frozen with fear and self-doubt, a barrage of different thoughts and feelings started to surface as I stood over the ball.

"Was it interlocking or was it overlapping?"

"What shot shape do I need to hit? I can't see it."

"Trouble down the right, trouble down the left."

"Are my competitors watching me? What will they think of me if I do not hit a great shot?"

"What am I doing here?!"

I tried to quiet my mind, yet thoughts continued pouring in. The clarity and confidence I once held on the golf course felt like a long-lost memory.

Only looking down the fairway out of habit, my eyes started to open to all the obstacles: the thick heather left and right of the fairway, the hazard that ran across the fairway at about 270 yards. I could see everything but the exact target or where I was trying to hit it.

If you stopped me during that moment and asked what I was trying to do with this golf ball, I wouldn't have been able to tell you.

I was blind to my surroundings because I was so lost inside my own thoughts. There is nothing worse than standing over the ball with a head full of swing thoughts, fears, and doubts. You cannot perform from a place of complexity.

When you are standing over the ball and thinking about technical details, swing positions and what you have been working on in the driving range, it all only gets in the way of your performance. When you are playing well and have a great scorecard in your hands, executing shot after shot, hitting fairways and greens and holing putts; whatever state you want to call this, "playing in the zone", going through a "purple patch", you are most likely just playing from stillness and presence.

Your mind will be quiet, you won't be worried about what position your swing needs to be in. The only thing you will be concerned about is the target and how to get the ball in the hole. When we were young and played sports growing up, we operated from this space. It was playful, fun, and simple.

The best way to practice this state of high performance doesn't come from beating hundreds of balls at the range. It doesn't come from having more lessons with your local pro, or from reading golf books like this one or understanding more about technical elements of the golf swing. It doesn't come from watching hours of YouTube videos of swing tutorials. The way you will enter this space is by developing the hardest skill this book will cover, which is to sit down with yourself and your thoughts and do absolutely nothing, otherwise known as mindful meditation.

This does not need to be complicated, but requires a conscious habit of taking time each day for just 10 minutes and practicing stillness and the non-judgmental observation of your thoughts and feelings. Habits are the compound interest of self-improvement. Turning up each day and sitting down to do your daily meditation will slow down your analytical thoughts and cage that monkey mind of yours. Eventually, this daily routine, done for long enough and done sincerely enough, becomes more than routine. It becomes a ritual and will serve you in more ways than just on the golf course.

When we all watched Tiger coming down the back nine on the Sunday of the 2019 Masters, was he thinking about swing thoughts? Was he thinking about a club position? No, he was completely present and in the moment. He had total awareness. Whilst his competitors made mistakes, missed shots, and agonised over what it would mean to them if they won the Masters, Tiger was poised and operating from a place of stillness and presence. With each stride he walked, each breath he took, and each swing he made, he was stillness. He was like a hawk, viewing everything from above whilst his competitors were on the front lines of a battle.

On my podcast, "Making A Club Champion", I have been fortunate enough to interview some of the best coaches around the world. At the end of each episode, I asked them for an actionable challenge – a specific drill or tip which they believe has changed their lives and their students for the better. The answer to 80% of these questions was meditation.

As hard as it is in the distracting realm of instant gratification and the constant accessibility of overwhelming information, the answer lies in tuning out the external influences. To step away, slow down, sit down, and be still with your thoughts and your breath.

So, to answer the original question; What to think about when over the ball? The answer is the shot at hand and being completely present with what you are trying to do with that shot. Anything else that comes into your mind or surfaces is noise and a distraction. Only when completely present with the shot can you enter a state of performance. If there was one takeaway from this book, it is that stillness is the key.

Takeaways...

1. Sitting down with your thoughts can be scary. If new to media-
    tion, I would suggest starting with guided meditation. There are
    some great apps such as Headspace or Calm. They are both free to
    download on your phone and are a great place to start. Another
    option that I have come across recently is "tapping meditation" or
    also known as EFT (Emotional freedom technique). It is a power-
    ful technique to release anxiety and release blocked energy.

    If you have been experimenting with meditation, or want to
    take it to the next level, drop the apps and sit in silence for 30-
    60 minutes and be at one with yourself and your breath, simply
    observing what comes up.

2. Three interviews from the, "Making A Club Champion" Podcast
    which will help you learn more about this:
    -   Ep 35: Jayne Storey – How to Play your Best Golf through
        Meditation, Breathing, and Quieting the Mind
    -   Ep 32: Lynn Marriott – Mental Game Golf Tips – What to
        Think When Over the Golf Ball
    -   Ep 30: Dr Joseph Parent – Mastering the Mental Game with
        Zen Golf

3. Some great books in this space outside of golf which I have found
    valuable and keep revisiting often:
    -   Stillness is the Key by Ryan Holiday
    -   The Power of Now: A Guide to Spiritual Enlightenment by
        Eckhart Tolle
    -   Deep Work by Carl Newport

LESSON NO. 4:

THE MOST POWERFUL LAW IN GOLF

Learning to ignore things is one of the great paths to inner peace.
—ROBERT J. SAWYER

I jump ship in Hong Kong and I make my way over to Tibet, So, I tell them I'm a pro jock, and who do you think they give me? The Dalai Lama, himself. Twelfth son of the Lama. The flowing robes, the grace, bald… striking. So, I'm on the first tee with him. I give him the driver. He hauls off and whacks one – big hitter, the Lama – long, into a ten-thousand foot crevasse, right at the base of this glacier. Do you know what the Lama says? Gunga galunga… gunga, gunga-lagunga. So we finish the eighteenth and he's gonna stiff me. And I say, "Hey, Lama, hey, how about a little something, you know, for the effort, you know." And he says, "Oh, uh, there won't be any money, but when you die, on your deathbed, you will receive total consciousness." So I got that goin' for me, which is nice.
—CARL SPACKLER

To be steady while the world spins around you. To act without frenzy. To hear only what needs to be heard. To possess quietude – exterior and interior – on command.
—RYAN HOLIDAY

To be a successful golf player, you must master your emotions the best you can.

This includes how you react to shots, the story you tell yourself standing on the opening tee in front of your club on a Saturday medal, and the way you think about yourself and your game in the loneliest moments on the course.

My original title of this book was going to be called: The War of Attrition: *A prolonged period of conflict during which each side seeks to gradually wear down the other by a series of small-scale actions.*

The game of golf is relentless. It is a game that will test you and wear you down.

So, it is how you manage your emotions during your round that will define your score.

It is all those tiny tests and moments when you will decide to either bend or break.

Golf somehow brings out all our emotions on the course. We get trapped in our own little world of thoughts and feelings, oblivious to the beauty around us.

Feeling stressed with work? Then you are likely to exhibit idiosyncrasies during your round. Feeling like you are high with life? You are likely to notice the lucky breaks and bounces that go your way. Your game will have more flow and rhythm, your swing will feel free, more effortless.

No two days are the same on the golf course. Your past successes are your biggest obstacles. Every battle on the course is different. You cannot assume that what has worked for you before will work today. You will always be hitting from different spots in different situations and conditions. You must learn and understand that each round is totally unique.

The secret is developing the skill of awareness and being present with yourself and your surroundings.

Starting to notice and pick up on the following and you will become aware of the state of mind you have on each day you play. What are you choosing to focus on? How does your body feel? What is the environment in which you are playing like today? How are your energy levels? Do you feel agitated or calm and relaxed?

By asking questions about yourself, you start to gather information and can paint a picture of the sort of game you will be tested with today. Some days we just wake up differently than others and it is up to us to notice these tendencies.

Warming up on the range, you notice for some mysterious reason that a draw is suiting your eye more. You may have played a five to seven-yard fade all season. Today is different, you are playing a three to four-yard draw. Being aware of these tendencies and insights is critical to your success and key to staying present on the course.

The "best" will gather these insights before they tee it up. That "ah-ha" moment when things start to click halfway through the round is too late.

The best are present with themselves and their thoughts before they arrive at the first tee. They sit in silence, they meditate. They are at "one" with themselves. When they get to the club, they will start to pick up on how their body is feeling during their warm-up on the range, how it is moving. The shot shapes they have for the day and what they will be working with. They start to get a sense and feel of where they are missing shots. How the club feels in their hands. How their body and mind are working with one another.

You are now standing on a hole knowing these insights about your game that have brought you on to the course this day. You are not being a stubborn golfer who is fighting with the past. Once where your mind was rigid, it is now open and flexible.

When you are aware of yourself, observe and take ownership of your performance on the course. It is the Club Championships, you have arrived at the club feeling more nervous than usual. Your heart is beating quicker. You are walking slightly faster, you go to the range and notice your rhythm is a little quicker than normal. You may notice your body is a little stiffer. When you notice these minute tendencies within yourself, you are about to deliberately slow everything down.

You start to breathe a little deeper, taking time with your routine. You now arrive on the first tee seeing and experiencing from the present moment. This is your Club Championships and you would really like to play with unprecedented positivity. You have not caught yourself in a flurry of emotions like your competitors. You are aware. You are calm and poised and ready to perform from a place of clarity. You have total presence.

During your round, you notice that your game is not quite there. You are not quite striking it and getting the ball where you want it to go. Knowing this, you start to take less aggressive lines off the tee. You play slightly more conservatively aiming to the wider parts of the fairway to put the ball in play. With your approach shots, you respect the flags and find greens, taking your pars and not making unforced errors.

As the round unfolds you make the turn and your playing partner makes a comment, "you're playing well aren't you, what score are you on?"

Their comment throws you a little and takes you out of the present moment. Your swing starts to get a little faster. Thanks to your playing partner, you now know you have a great score going, you have the potential to win your club championships. Instead of reacting to this, you pause and reflect. You make a mental note that you are playing well, and you do have a great score going, but this is far from over. You inform yourself to slow down, be still, get back to focusing on one shot at a time. One breath at a time.

You are now standing on the 17th hole. A thought creeps into your mind. "Two pars to finish, I think I have got this." You picture yourself lifting the trophy, with your name engraved, in front of your mates at the club with celebratory drinks.

Instead of holding onto this thought like a child holding onto a balloon, you once again appreciate that it has surfaced, take a step back from it and you gently unclench the thought and let it go into the wind. You replace the internal dialogue by imagining you had a caddy standing next to you. You go through the shot at hand with one another, making sure you have thought about all the options before you stand over the ball.

A great boxer who walks into the ring is not going to start throwing haymakers to win within the first round. They will carefully study and assess their opponent. See how they react to a right jab, a left jab. They will observe the test are they dealing with today and build a strategy to overcome it.

Remove yourself from playing the game in your own little world. Think that you are viewing your game from the outside in, rather than the inside out. This way you are being less reactive to given situations, seeing each shot as its own unique shot.

Be aware of your game and notice the patterns. Awareness is freedom.

The secret is to be aware.

Takeaways...

Our minds on the golf course can sometimes feel like muddy water. To see through it, we have to let things settle.

If you are interested in the philosophy side of golf, here are a couple of resources.

1. Meditate

This moment we are experiencing right now is a gift, that is why we call it "present." Being "present" is a demanding task. It may be the hardest thing in the world.

Meditating for just 10 mins a day can have wonderful effects. Apps like Calm or Headspace are a great place to start. This is a long-term practice with subtle wins to help you create stillness.

2. Limit Your Inputs & Cultivate Silence

Too many inputs can cause information overload, complexity, and anxiety. Try going on a "low information diet" That means no texting, no calls, no email, no news, no Facebook, no Instagram.

If we want to think better, have more insights, breakthroughs, or ideas, we need to seize the moments of stillness. By limiting your inputs and turning down the external volume, you can access a deeper awareness of what's going on around you.

Pulling the ripcord on a lifetime of habits is probably not the easiest long-term strategy. If your inputs are overwhelming, you could start off with one day a week where you say no to any internal stimuli. Choose a day that works for you and allow only nature and face-to-face interactions.

3. Empty The Mind/Journaling

Whatever you face, don't make it harder by overthinking, by needless doubts, or by second-guessing.

Instead of letting racing thoughts run unchecked or leaving half-baked assumptions unquestioned, cage the monkey mind on paper each morning by offloading all those internal thoughts, to-do lists, and emotional baggage.

Putting your own thinking down on paper lets you see it from a distance. It is effectively emptying your trash. Keep your mind clean and clear.

LESSON NO. 5:

THE PERFECT 100 BALL ROUTINE AND THE TIGER WOODS DRIVING RANGE DRILL

If you can't beat them, outwork them.
—BEN HOGAN

What 20% of effort results in 80% of time wasted in golf? The range.

A place where there is no routine/structure.

A field with no outcomes, an unlimited number of balls, and time to spend tinkering around grooving in bad habits and swing changes.

We feel like it is set up for success and a place to get better, but without discipline, it is set up for disaster.

The key to spending time on the range is installing good habits and routines that implement a combination of technical, skill development, pressure and performance-related outcomes to make you feel accountable.

Making this separation between the two when practicing is vital, "playing golf" and "playing golf swing" are two different skill sets. Blending the two together is when practice time becomes ineffective and bad habits creep in.

Playing golf swing is when you're focused internally. You're thinking about the pieces of your swing – shoulder turn, wrist angles, etc. You're not thinking about the shot itself.

Playing golf is getting the ball into the hole in as few strokes as possible. In this mindset, you're focused on all the things that affect the shot – lie, wind, and what you want the ball to do. The focus is on the shot at hand, not the swing.

"If you were to stop one of the best players in the world in the middle of their practice session, they would be able to tell you exactly what they are working on and why they are doing it.

They might even be able to break that down and talk about a shot that they are going to face this week, or a shot they hit last week that didn't feel right.

The best players have a feedback loop that enables them to do that. They are able to pinpoint what is going on in their game very accurately and work on it.

Practicing for the sake of practicing and without the purpose of trying to improve either technique, skill, or performance. You should not be on the range." (Ep 8 on MakingAClubChampion.com - Laurie Canter – Life on the European Tour)

The Perfect 100 Balls

You can do this with a different size basket of balls but in this case, we are going to use 100 balls as an example.

First 25 Balls: Warm Up

When you get your basket of 100 balls, pour roughly 1/4 (25 balls) into the tray. The first 25 balls have no target in mind. Just try and get a feel of the club in your hands and a sense of how your swing and body are moving on this day.

Have fun with the shots, be creative. Play a few straight shots, try and hit some big draws, some big fades, exaggerate the feelings on how your body is moving. Go through your bag with a couple of different clubs. Be present with the feelings you have that day. Use these first 25 balls to warm up and get loose with the swing you have today.

25 - 50 Balls: Technical drill, something you are working on with your coach

Once you have finished, pour roughly another 25 balls into the tray. In this next batch, you are going to work on a technical drill. This may be with a training aide or specific movement you have been working on with your coach that you are trying to ingrain.

Do not worry about the outcome or where the ball is going. Have total detachment from the results. During these 25 balls, you are training your mind and body to work on specific movements that will put your body and club in better positions.

50 - 75 Balls: Pick a Target

For the next 25, it is time to start putting what you have worked on technically by hitting balls at targets on the range. Whether it is a green, flag, or yardage marker, put what you have been working on to the test and get some feedback on how it feels when hitting at the target. Let go of your swing thoughts and focus solely on the ball aiming at the target. During this stage, you can keep hitting shots at the same target to groove in what you have been working on with your swing.

75 - 100 Balls: Implementing Pressure, Consequences, and Keeping Score

In this final stage of your practice session, you are putting your game to the test. You have now warmed up, worked on some technical drills, tested how that felt and now you are going to see how you perform. As if you had a scorecard in your hand and recreating a tournament like a scenario. This will put you under a bit of pressure and under the pump.

Here are a couple of games/drills you can play to test your game.

1. Dave Alred - The How Many To Drill
Pick two targets, on the range such as a flag, yardage markers, or sides of the green on the range. If testing your iron game, pick two targets about the width of a green. If testing your long game/driver, pick two objects that are the width of a fairway.

In this game, you are going to be testing how many shots it takes you to hit five balls in a row, between your two targets. You have to start again if you fail to hit it inside your intended targets. Make a note, how many balls it takes you with each club. (Ep 12 on MakingA-ClubChampion.com - Dave Alred - The Pressure Principles)

2. Dr Brian Hemmings - Practicing Quality and Patience
When I first started playing golf at age 13, I was lucky enough to be coached by Dr. Brian Hemmings (Ep 15 on MakingAClubChampion.com). For the past two decades, he was the lead psychologist to the England golf team, working with the likes of Danny Willett, Chris Wood and Ross Fisher. I made a note of a range tip in one of my journals after my first lesson with him.

Take your remaining 25 balls and instead of pouring them into the tray, take them to the back of the range. Pick a target, find the yardage, and go through your whole routine with each ball.

In this drill, you are going to be hitting different targets with different clubs for each ball and track the dispersion of each shot in a journal.

After each shot, write down the yardage and how far you missed it, long, short left and right.

As your basket of the balls is now at the back of the range, you will have to walk back to your bag and start the whole process again. It is a great drill that practices discipline and patience.

The 9 Shots - Tiger Woods Driving Range Drill

I am always trying to shape the ball.

—JACK NICKLAUS.

Tiger has always been my golfing hero. This is how Tiger Woods spends his time on the range and how you too can practice like one of the world's best-ever players.

There are only nine *proper* shots that a golfer needs to master. They are as follows: the high draw, high straight and high fade. The stock draw, stock fade, and stock straight. The low draw, low fade, and low straight.

Tiger Woods, arguably one of the greatest iron game players, can flight the ball and shape it better than most using this shot-making skill. If you have got control of your golf ball, you can start attacking flags. If you can attack flags with confidence, you are going to score better.

If you are unable to hit certain shot shapes you will be limited to how close you can hit your shots to the hole on the golf course. Golf can be a difficult game if you do not have control of your shot-making.

You need to be able to hit certain shot shapes to break 80 consistently. To consistently break 70, you will need to be able to access more than one stock shot. Does your ball flight match up with your golfing goals? How many shots do you have in your bag which you can consistently rely on?

How to Play the 9 Shot Game

The 9 Shots is a game for you to practice on the range. The more you practice this drill, the more confident you will feel on the course. Having more ability to control your ball flight and being able to work the ball into areas on the course and greens will set you up for success.

You're not only trying to hit all nine ball flights correctly, you're also getting them to land in a specified target area.

What Clubs to Practice with?

Mid irons to long irons.

You are not going to be able to shape the ball with your wedges like you can with your mid to long irons. As this is a constant skill and test on your game, I would suggest using the same club each time for this drill. A six or seven iron is perfect for this drill.

What's the target?

Say, if your seven iron goes 150 yards. Imagine a 9 box grid above the 150-yard marker.

You do not want the ball to cross the center lines. It is better to miss the shot on the outside of the lines, otherwise draws become hooks and fades becomes slices.

With longer clubs, your target area for a successful shot should be slightly larger, perhaps within 10 yards of a specific target on the range.

How to work through the 9 shots?

Starting on the bottom right with the low draw. As soon as you hit a low draw that lands in your target area, move on to the quadrant above. In a right-handed case, medium draw then high draw. Then do the low straight, medium straight, high straight and finally low fade, medium fade, and high fade. Going in this format means you cover three-shot shapes at a time.

There are two games that will help keep you accountable and introduce pressure. This exercise will provide valuable information and data about your game, the shots you can hit and more importantly highlighting the shots you cannot hit. Use these drills to build confidence, improve your shot-making and make better choices on the golf course.

Game number #1: 9 balls, 9 shots and 9 points (0-12 hcp)

The first game creates a sense of pressure and feeling of having to execute right from the first shot you hit. This game is designed for the lower handicapper.

On the course, you only get one shot and one try to hit that shot. If you can hit all these shots when it matters on the first attempt, you can call yourself a player.

If you have these nine shots grooved into your game, you can work the ball into areas of the course which eliminate risk and maximize your potential to shoot lower scores. If you can play all these 9 shots on demand, you will be able to hit more fairways, more greens and attack flags which you were not able to get to before, leading play with confidence to shoot lower scores. Keep track of your scores and go back and review your weak shots. Play as many games as you want on the given day at a range session. Keep working on this drill until you can master the 9 shots with 9 balls, and get your 9 points.

Game #2: How Many Till (12hcp+)

In this game, you are counting how many attempts it takes to play this shot until executed. Even the best players in the world would struggle to do the perfect 9, so if you are just starting to outplay the "How Many Till" game:

Write down how many shots it has taken until you have executed the shot.

This exercise really highlights your strengths and weaknesses with your shot making.

LESSON NO. 6:

HOW TO WIN AND GET WHAT YOU WANT FROM THE GAME

I have never achieved what I thought was a success. Golf to me is a business, a livelihood in doing the thing that I like to do. I don't like glamour. I just like the game.

—BEN HOGAN

The key to pursuing excellence is to embrace an organic, long-term learning process, and not to live in a shell of static, safe mediocrity. Usually, growth comes at the expense of previous comfort or safety.

—JOSHUA WAITZKIN

The tighter we cling to an identity, the harder it becomes to grow beyond it.

—JAMES CLEAR

It was one of the proudest moments in all my golfing experience: being one of six to be selected to represent GB&I against America. Playing 20 matches in 21 days - against the best talent on the east coast. We toured all the way from South Carolina to New York, playing some of the finest US Open Courses and Private Country clubs like Pine Valley, Merrion and Baltusrol, to name a few.

From single figures to plus handicaps, and the likes of Nick Faldo and Rollan Rafferty's son's making up the squad, we were a strong team on paper: all hungry, young, and mad about golf. We were 10 matches into the tour and had just finished another team win. After a few celebratory Arnold Palmer's (a refreshing beverage popular in America; half iced tea and half lemonade served over ice) sitting on the balcony catching the last rays of the sun disappearing over the 18th green, we jumped on the team bus and made our way up the coast to our accommodation for the night. This usually involved staying with a local family or a member of the country club where we were playing next.

On the drive up, our coach turned off the radio and asked all of us to define our golfing goals. As we went around members of the team each player defined what they wanted to achieve in the game.

"To win my Club Championships"

"To get selected for my County"

"To get my handicap to plus 3"

"To turn pro"

When it came to a certain member of the team, his response silenced the bus.

"To be world number one"

I think the whole bus thought he was joking, but he said again with a serious face,

"To be world number one, that is what I want to achieve".

After he said it a second time, with a stern look in his eyes, we didn't question him.

Early that afternoon, when we were all relaxing and enjoying Arnold Palmers. We had a team picture taken after the round, but there was one member of the team missing. That person was Matt Wallace; he was on the range practicing.

Matt set his goals and dreams far greater than anyone else on the team. He knew what he wanted to achieve, had a strong compelling vision that he deeply believed in, and he relentlessly chipped away at to make it happen.

If you're looking to win and get what you want from this game, set your vision higher than anyone else. Then get prepared to work.

Takeaways... The A - Z - B Drill

This is a simple and effective drill to keep asking yourself and journaling on. Grab yourself a pen, a glass of your favorite beverage, and a journal. Ask yourself these three questions:

A) Where are you now with your game?

Z) What are your dreams/visions with the game?

B) What is the very next thing you need to do to get you one step closer to your vision?

Once you have defined the end goal, let go of it. The only thing you need to know and always be focused and working on, is B.

LESSON NO. 7:

HOW TO HIT MORE FAIRWAYS

Do what you fear and fear disappears.
—DAVID JOSEPH SCHWARTZ

Golf is not a game of good shots. It's a game of bad shots.
—BEN HOGAN

Stop fraternizing with the help Gilmore. Just hit your ball... if you can find it.
—Shooter McGavin

Same thoughts always lead to the same choices, same choices lead to the same behavior and the same behaviors lead to same experiences and the same experiences produce the same emotions and these emotions drive the very same thoughts.
—JOE DISPENZA

I had the yips off the tee for two years; it was painful.
The only net benefit of having the yips with the driver is that it gives you a great opportunity to improve your chipping. You learn to fight and grind for your score every hole, playing from lies and places around the course that not even the greenkeepers have experienced. But this is not fun and not how the game should be played. My handicap tripled in two seasons in the wrong direction, going from plus one to two and struggling to break 80 most of the time. Golf is far easier being played from the middle of the fairway.

One of the great lessons college golf taught me was from my college golf captain. He was a lefty that had the game and mentality to get the ball around the course and win tournaments. After several rounds with him when I first arrived in North Carolina, he gave me some radically honest feedback on my game:

"You can't have a what the f*** shot in your bag, and you've got one".

It was the blunt and simple truth. Or as another chap called Ben Hogan put it *"This is a game of misses. The guy who misses the best is going to win."*

The definition of a "what the f*** shot" is splitting the first three fairways down the middle, and then standing on the fourth and knocking it so far out of bounds that you would have to get in your car to find it.

If you have a *"what the f*** shot"* in your bag, you will be caught out. This will happen when: you are faced with a tough driving hole, a hole doesn't fit your eye, there is, "out of bounds" or water running down the side of the hole, you are coming down the last couple of holes with an opportunity to win, you have a great scorecard in your hand and the pressure is on. It will rise like the phoenix and present itself in a quick hook left or carve right into the unknown.

Not finding fairways results in you being left four to five footers for most of your round, that is if you are lucky and have an exceptional wedge game. When you start missing those four to five-foot putts for par, which you will, the rails will start to come off and you become mentally worn down. You will get tired of grinding away and when you are coming down the last four holes of the back nine, you will have used all your mental decision units up and will make sloppy mistakes, resulting in more drop shots. The result: you will get in your car, drive home and enter the mental sabotage of questioning, "why do I keep playing this stupid game?"

When I was at the lowest point in my game, I eventually moved into a crippling phase of having the yips off the tee and the yips around the greens with my wedges and putter. A mentor of mine, Malcolm Lewis, Silver Medal winner at The Open Championship at Troon 1982, put it wonderfully: This is when *"an overdone strength can eventually become a weakness"*. What eventually happens is that your game becomes so reliant on your chipping and putting the pressure chamber breaks, and once where you had fluidity you now have rigidity. Voila, the yips move into your short game.

When you have problems off the tee with being unable to find fairways, you most likely have tried to overcomplicate things moving the ball both ways, which has resulted in a two way miss. This means you standing up on a tee box and not knowing if it is going left or right. You are in what we call *"no man's land"*.

If struggling to put the ball in play. These are the secrets and insights I discovered going through the yips and moving back to finding more fairways. Note, these were not the technical changes I made, but more mental and strategic. Yips can be kick-started by technical issues, but the damage will be mainly psychological.

1. Change your internal dialogue

The first step in changing any element of your game is to change the mindset that goes with it. The internal dialogue: the story you tell yourself and how you define certain elements of your game, is very important. If the internal story is not an empowering one, this is the first thing you need to change. So, when you are taking your practice swings looking down the hole or standing over your ball with the driver in your hands, listen closely to the story you tell yourself and the thoughts you are experiencing.

If you define yourself as a poor driver of the golf ball, it does not matter how much you technically improve, if you stand over the ball with a disempowering story you will struggle to find fairways. The mind and body work hand in hand when playing golf - a change in that internal story to a more empowering one is the best place to start in order to challenge thoughts which are not based on fact. (More on this in lesson no.5)

For this, I would try affirmations. Every time you have the driver in your hand, you can repeat the same phrase of your choosing over and over again. Here are some empowering affirmation examples:

"I am a great driver of the golf ball."

"I love hitting my driver straight down the middle of the fairways."

"I am the fairway finder."

Like doing lines when you misbehaved at school, you could also write these down in your golfing journal. The power is in the repetition of positive affirmations.

2. Take one side of the fairway out of play

Different holes will require you to move the ball in different ways. Doglegs right to left set up for the player who likes to draw the ball. Dogleg left to right sets up well for the faders of the ball. Exceptional drivers of the ball and can shape the ball to the hole. If you are struggling to find fairways, and have been for a while, forget trying to shape the ball both ways off the tee. *Take one side of the fairway out of play.* Pick a shot shape and flight and do not deviate from that.

The best way to pick your shot shape is to think about how you see the ball move through the air when you are under pressure. Whatever that is, trust and respect that shot.

I spent 10+ years trying to draw the ball right to left. But I just can't do it well enough when I am under pressure and want to put the ball in play. The shot I naturally see is the ball starting down the left side and sliding back into the middle of the fairway. The right to left shot is my ego. It is the shot that I desire to hit, but it is not effective for me and my game. Do not make the same 10-year stubborn mistake I made. Take one side of the fairway out of play, get back to hitting one-shot shape over and over again.

3. Having a "go-to fairway finder"

This is when you look down at a hole and you see nothing. You can't picture your shot flight or shape, or which side of the fairway to hit on; nothing is coming to you. In fact, all you think about is just getting this shot over and done with. This is when having a *"go-to fairway finder"* comes into play. This is a shot where you sacrifice a bit of distance, but you know that it is going to find the fairway.

For me, it is a driver or 3 wood off the deck. I aim down the left side of the fairway or even rough and hit a hard power fade. The confidence I get from this shot is knowing that this ball is not going left. This shot always complies with rule number 2) *Taking one side of the fairway out of play.* When using this shot, identify the large part of the fairway and swing with confidence to that intended target.

LESSON NO. 8:

HOW TO DEVELOP THE HABIT OF PRACTICING CONSISTENTLY

There are no shortcuts in the quest for perfection.
—BEN HOGAN

Life is not a dress rehearsal. If you are not doing it now, you are not doing it.
—MY DAD

Not enough people do what they say they are going to do. Words do not mean an awful lot, it is your actions which are the key. Stop bullshitting yourself. If you want to do something, make a plan to do it, but actually, carry it out. Be accountable to yourself. So you can say to yourself." I said I was going to do it and I did it, that then transfers onto the golf course.
—KARL MORRIS - (Ep 16 on MakingAClubChampion.com)

Great outcomes are a direct product of extra effort.
—UNKNOWN

Back in 1965, Sports Illustrated said I was going to be the next Arnold Palmer.
—CHUBBS

Work is much more fun than fun.
—NOEL COWARD

We don't rise to the level of our expectations, we fall to the level of our training.
—ARCHILOUS

At age 12, I set the grand audacious goal of playing in the 2010 Ryder Cup at Celtic Manor.

Why? Because the course was not far from my parent's home. I ate, drank, and dreamt golf. I had eight years to earn my Tour Card and finish high enough in the order of merit to earn the spot. As lofty as it was, that was what I was going after.

I have always been a goal setter, both on and off the golf course.

I have always believed in big goals: grand and unflinching ones.

The main problem with goal setting is we either don't meet our goals and see ourselves as a failure, or we meet our goals inflated and have to rebuild and define what's next.

When we set grand and presumptuous goals, sometimes even the smallest tasks seem to be put off for another day. Ambitious goals also seem to emphasize a delay in happiness. Only when I achieve "X" will I be happy. Too often, we convince ourselves that massive success requires massive action.

What we fail to realize is the continual tiny improvements each day when reviewing back over the course of a month, a year, a decade, really move the needle in terms of growth. If we got one percent better each day for one year, we would end up thirty-seven times better. Small, smart choices + consistency + time = radical growth.

If you eat an unhealthy meal today, it isn't going to move the needle that much. It's the accumulation of many unhealthy meal choices every day for a month. Our small choices can compound into toxic results. We get what we repeat.

Living in a day-to-day, goal-oriented atmosphere is like a pressure chamber, it's exhausting and mentally draining. You live in a state of nearly continuous failure until you meet your goal before you restart the process again.

When playing college golf in America, I was putting all sorts of pressure on my game by setting more and more lofty goals. I was so desperate to get better each season, trying to force the process, my game started to break down and suffer. It wasn't until one afternoon when I asked the following questions: *What would it look like if I did the opposite? What If I completely ignored my goals and focused only on a system instead, would I succeed?*

A system automates to take care of the process, enabling you to reach your capabilities, going above and beyond your goals. It is also more fun, more rewarding, realistic, and flexible.

If goals are the macro, systems are the micro. Systems are about creating a repeatable set of actions and recurring processes of showing up. Systems serve to motivate with rituals and routines.

Our actions are the one thing that we are in control of. Setting ambitious goals in all areas of your life is great but the next step is to detach yourself being fixated away from them and then shift into a systems-based approach.

Here is the difference between systems and goals.

Example of some golfing goals

- If you are a coach, your goal might be to take your player/ college team to win a major championship or tour event.
- If you are a player, your goal might be to win a major championship, earn your tour card, win your club championships, or play off single figures.
- If you are a caddy, your goal might be to get a bag on a junior tour, then move your way up to the PGA/European Tour. Then get your first tour/major win.

Goals rely on willpower. Willpower is like putting the doughnut in front of the child, who will always eat it, no matter how great the reward! Goals are like new year resolutions: you get off to a fast start, then you lose motivation and start to forget why you are doing it.

Replacing goals with systems makes things easier.

Example of some golfing systems:

- I am one hell of a putter; I hit 50 putts on the putting rail each night
- I am an amazing driver of the ball; I practice the Dave Alred "how many too" drill on the driving range three times a week
- I am deadly around the greens; I practice with my wedges every day and do the Dave Pelz short game test once a week
- I am mentally tough and can make clear decisions on the course because I turn up and meditate every day

The idea is simply not to let a single day pass without doing something, however tiny, towards getting better at a certain element of your game. This gentle shift in your approach starts to affect how you define yourself. Let's take putting as an example.

If you practiced 50 putts on the putting rail each night, you would start to develop a greater stroke and roll the ball better on the greens. When you roll the ball better, you get more confidence, and you start to hole more putts. When you hole more putts, you label and identify yourself as "a great putter." That is when you become deadly on the greens. You see results, you reform your identity, and you have set a new belief.

Another element of showing up and doing the work is to be flexible along the way to achieving your goals. German philosopher Schopenhauer posited a chess analogy to demonstrate how goal-setting can be unrealistic. When playing chess, we start out with a plan, but our plan is affected by the inclinations of the other player. Our plan must modify itself constantly, to the point that, as we carry it out, several of its fundamental features are unrecognizable. To stick blindly to the same goals would be to deny that a second, independent player was at the board. So, no matter what you do, control your effort, stay flexible and open and give it your all. The rewards come later.

Writing this book was a goal. I put it off for years. It was only when I applied a system of "write every day from 9am-12pm", that my goal became a reality. It is so simple but so effective: Just put your head down, forget your goals, and get to work.

Goals are good for setting a direction, but systems are best for making progress in the long term. It's easy to underestimate the value of making small improvements on a daily basis. Reward the effort, instead of achievement. The secret to getting better year after year is to play the long game. Think systems, not goals.

LESSON NO. 9:

COURSE NAVIGATION AND STRATEGY - HOW TO MOVE THE BALL AROUND THE COURSE LIKE A PRO

The most important shot in golf is the next one.

You have to give careful thought to every shot. Every shot sets up what you are going to do next. Every shot has to be placed correctly. Don't ever just hit a shot without thinking it through.

Placing the ball in the right position for the next shot is 80-percent of winning golf.

—BEN HOGAN

Some of the best golfers I have played with do not always appear to hit the best shots. They sometimes hit the ball down the edges of the fairways and hit it away from the pins. After the round, I have been left scratching my head at the bar, thinking, "How did they just shoot a 69! They didn't even hit a great shot!"

As my handicap started to come down, I started to compete with better players around the world. The ones that scored well time and time again just seemed to know how to get the ball around the course better. They didn't always have the best swings, but they knew how to score. These are golfers that have a great golfing IQ.

Golf is about patience, strategy, putting yourself in position, then seeing what you can do in those moments. The golf course is set up to catch you out. Instead of thinking about course management think in terms of course navigation, your job is to navigate the ball around the course as effectively as possible. Good course navigation entails minimizing risk and taking advantage of opportunities at the same time.

These are some of the best secrets I have learned from watching and competing against the very best.

1. Find the Uphill Putt

We are taught to think about a target and focus on one shot at a time, but great golfers view the game more like a chess match or a game of snooker. You should always be thinking one shot ahead to make your next shot as easy as possible.

When we look down at a golf hole, we always want to keep this as the number one rule in our minds and ask ourselves: What is the easiest shot I can give myself next?

This all starts with "find the uphill putt."

When we start from the hole and work back, we start to see a strategic plan of how to play the hole in front of us. Unless you like slippery downhill knee jerkers, an uphill put is always the end goal. So, when we create our plan to play any hole, we want to work back from that intention.

An uphill putt left to right or right to left is going to give us the best possible chance of getting the ball in the hole. We can be firm, aggressive and if we give ourselves 18 chances to make putts, we are going to save ourselves a ton of strokes.

If playing at your home club, you know how certain greens slope and the places not to leave the ball. If you do not, start becoming more aware, take notes of where the flat and uphill zones are.

If it is a new course, keep an eye on the contours and edges of the green. Even from a distance, subtleties of the green design will give you indicators of places to leave the ball.

When playing a practice round for a tournament, buy the course-book and mark all of the flat and uphill sections on the green. You can shade, highlight, or cross these sections in to make it clear that these are your landing zones.

So, when next looking down at a par 3, 4, or 5, ask yourself:

Where do I need to hit this ball to give myself the uphill putt? This is your new target and landing zone, not the flag.

The next lesson will help with how to hit the ball in these zones.

2. Identify your Landing Zone:

It takes discipline to hit away from your targets and away from the center points of the fairway and pins. Pin positions can be tucked behind bunkers, over lakes, front or back of the greens. Most golfers think in terms of straight lines. Tee box to flag. It's now time to shift your focus and think of angles.

When watching golf on television next, if you listen closely to the commentators, they will say things like; "That's a good leave" or, "That's not a bad miss."

If you listen really closely when Tiger plays, he will say to his cad-dy, Joey, "left the angle". It may appear a stray shot for us viewers, but the very best at the game are seeing it differently.

So, when standing on the tee, your first point of focus should be finding the pin. From that, you can decide where you need to put the ball on the fairway to give yourself the very best chance to create the angel to hit the ball under the hole.

Your playing partners may not even think you are hitting it that well when you hit it deliberately down the right or left side of the fairways rather down the middle. But you have thought one shot ahead. What appeared to be a stray shot has just created an angle for you to attack the pin.

Leave your ego at the table and stick to the game plan. When you are standing on the tee box of a par 4 or par 5 ask yourself the following question:

> *Where is the widest landing zone on the fairway to give myself the best angel to be able to hit the ball under the pin?*

3. Know Thy Strengths: Hit into Your Numbers

Hitting your tee shots into yardages which you do not feel comfortable at is the easiest way to make hard work of your time spent out on the course. We all have strengths and weaknesses in our game, but if you keep hitting into spots off the tee and leaving yourself awkward yardages which you do not feel comfortable with, then you are going to make this game hard work.

A much easier technique is to leave yourself numbers all day which you feel comfortable with.

Out of all the yardages in my bag, my dispersion is the greatest at 160-175 yards. Why struggle during your round to leave yourself a number you know you are weak at? Hitting a 3 wood off on a par 4 or laying up on a par 5 to leave myself this number is not playing to my strengths. Knowing this information and data about your game is key.

I would much prefer to find a wide landing zone further down the fairway and play aggressively into that and leave myself 110-130 yards, even from the rough. From there, I know I can take advantage of hitting it close from this range, with this yardage, as I have the tightest dispersion.

It is much better to pour gasoline over your strengths than fix your weaknesses. Sounds simple, but playing with golfers from around the world, most of them ignore this rule.

Hitting into specific positions on the course and giving yourself yardages, where you are exceptionally strong, is a deadly weapon for you to take advantage of on the course.

To do this, you must know your dispersion at every yardage. When caddying on the European Tour, I worked with a couple of players that helped me develop a system to calculate dispersion and proximity to the hole at each given yardage. If you do not fancy spending $30k on a TrackMan, The Score Better Journal: Track Analyze and Improve Your Game, is a great alternative. After a couple of entries, you can see which areas of your game are strong and which are weak.

4. Find the Flat Lie on the Fairways

This rule won't apply to all holes. But there will be certain holes on the course where certain sides of the fairway will be better landing zones than others. Imagine playing on the par 4 10th at Augusta. Failing to get the ball down the left side of the fairway will result in hitting your second shot from a hanging lie into a narrow green. It is keyholes like this which demonstrate when it is important to identify the flat sides of the fairway.

Once you have identified your landing zone, leaving yourself a yardage that you are strong at, you now need to ask:

"What side of the landing zone will leave me the flattest lie?"

Nothing is harder than working the ball onto the green from a hanging lie or a ball way below your feet. A fairway can look like a large runway strip to land on. But the great players who score well divide that landing zone into more specific areas.

The secret is to identify the area on the fairway which will give you the best chance of hitting your next shot under the hole and leave yourself an uphill putt. Depending on the course, there may only be a few holes where this comes into play. But it is worth making a note of these holes and being aware of the lie in mind.

Golf holes are designed to have strengths and weaknesses. Weaknesses of golf holes are the wide landing zones, flat stretches on the fairway and bailout areas around the green. Identify them, play to your strengths, and bring the course to its knees.

5. Pin Positions: The Rule of Six

Golf courses usually set up their pin positions with six easy, six medium and six sucker pins. Splitting up the course in this way will help you break down which pins are there to avoid, respect and attack. Players who attack pins are like greedy gamblers at the casino; great players wait for their run and stay patient.

With this in mind, we take a golf course from having 18 holes to a specific game plan. When standing over a tee shot on a par 3, or an approach to a par 4/par 5, you can ask yourself the following questions:

"Which pin is this - easy, medium or sucker?"
"Am I in a position of strength on the fairway to attack this pin?"
"Am I in a landing zone, in an area of strength for my game?"
"Am I in the best possible position to attack this pin and leave it under the hole?"

If you do not like the six rule, you can use the Darren Clarke Traffic Light Rule, and ask yourself, "Is this pin position a green light (all systems go), orange light, (be respectful and play 15-20 yards away from the flag) or red light hit to a bailout area under the hole."

Takeaways...

When implementing this strategy out on the course for the first time, really exaggerate these principles to begin with and over time you can tighten them up.

Deliberately hitting the ball short or long of the flag to give yourself an uphill putt or chip is a skill. Start to implement and practice it.

Are you seeing the hole as it is and just trying to hit straight lines to the pins? Or are you practicing your craft of deliberately moving the ball around the course to create your best possible angles and outcomes?

Throughout the course of the round, the game will feel less of a struggle. You are having to grind less to fight for your score as you are rarely out of position. You are making the work appear easy. The secret is to think of course navigation instead of course management.

LESSON NO. 10:

HOW TO KEEP YOUR ENERGY LEVELS UP THROUGHOUT THE ROUND

Let food be thy medicine.
—HIPPOCRATES

I believe nicotine plus caffeine equals protein.
—JOHN DALY

One of the biggest takeaways I learned from caddying on the European Tour was how meticulous the pros were at doing the small things.

Everything they did was a standard above what I had seen when growing up in the amateur game. No stone was left unturned, they prepped for their success, there was no wastage. Everything was squeezed out of their performance like a formula one racing car.

However...

One thing I did notice that rang alarm bells, was off the course.

After the day's play and maybe some further practice time on range, we would normally go out for dinner at a local restaurant with a couple of other players, or head to a supermarket and cook up a dinner in the apartments.

With such knowledge about their games and swing, it came as a bit of shock to see how much they didn't question what they were fueling their bodies with. Some of the players' choices in foods captured my attention. Evening meals consisted of loading up on high carbohydrate meals like pizza, pasta, or a bowl of chips and sometimes the odd bottle of red. For breakfast it would be bowls of cereal and oats drizzled in honey. The worst I saw was one of the players sitting down for breakfast with a loaf of white bread and a jar of Nutella.

I couldn't wrap my head around how these players had a degree's worth of knowledge on their swing and how to knock the ball around the course in the fewest shots possible. Yet, they did not take the same level of research into the foods that were fueling their performance. During the rounds, it would be the same: glorified candy bars masked as energy/protein bars.

Since I was young, I have always experimented with nutrition with performance in mind.

Some of my nutrition experiments include the following.

- 2016 - I decided to run two Iron Man entirely on coconut oil and cashew butter in Hawaii and Napa Valley.
- 2017 - I took this one stage further and spent a year in ketosis, this is where you are using fat for energy instead of carbohydrates and sugar. Each morning I would add two tablespoons of grass-fed butter and something called brain octane oil (Medium Chain Triglyceride) into my coffee and blend it. I would not then eat until 5-7 pm in the evening. Where again I would eat a meal that was made up of 70-80% fat, 10-20% protein and the rest carbs. I would have to pee on "keto sticks" each morning to check if I was in a ketogenic state.
- 2018 – I went fully vegan.

- 2019 – I experimented with intermittent fasting for 16 hours a day for a year.
- 2019-2021 – I implemented the Paleo diet or also known as the caveman diet, and then started my own Paleo nutrition company - called, "No Ordinary Moments".

I have tested the body like a guinea pig to find what foods work for me over the years. Why? It was clear that certain foods contributed to my success and others were taking me away from my performance, health, and mindset.

During experiments and setting up my own nutrition company, I have learned how the food industry works and how they market their products to make profit. A schema is a cognitive framework or concept that helps organize and interpret information. Big food companies use these all the time to help sell their products and churn a profit. Here are some examples of sticky schemes used in the breakfast marketplace. Schemas can be useful because they allow us to take shortcuts in interpreting the vast amount of information.

- "Fuel for big days" Weetabix
- "Nothing is better for thee, than me" Quaker Oats
- "They're Gr-r-reat!" Frosted Flakes
- "Have a break. Have a Kit-Kat" KitKat
- "The Breakfast of Champions" Wheaties

Have we ever stopped to question any of these? Or do we take these powerful marketing messages for what they are?

I was always told by my parents and other health-related mediums that starting your day off with a bowl of oats and milk was the healthiest way to start your day. But what if we step back and question these assumptions, see it more as a simple experiment with cause and effect. Would we arrive at the same conclusions?

- Hypothesis "Take oats for breakfast with milk and a dash of honey"
- Result "Do I feel energized hours after or do I feel I am feeling hungry again?"

Using this simple example around two to three hours later I would always feel hungry again and be craving something to eat. It was the craving that rang alarm bells, why do I feel like this only a matter of hours after I have eaten. I was not energized but always looking for the next food to top me up. I felt like I was riding a roller coaster of highs and lows with my energy levels.

In 2013 I did my strength and conditioning qualification in San Francisco, taking a deep dive into training and nutrition. I quickly learned that the diet I was on had me on an insulin roller coaster. Having a bowl of oats for breakfast with skimmed milk and some honey was effectively having a bowl of sugar to start the day. To get back up to a high, I would have a sandwich at lunch, and then once I had plummeted from that high carbohydrate meal I would indulge in some rice, pasta with some protein of choice. All sounds very healthy, but I was left feeling drained and zapped each day.

Another concept that we believe in as a society is that when going out to a restaurant or being entertained at someone's house, we determine the success of a meal by the statement, "that meal was absolutely delicious, I am so full".

You never really want to feel full after you have eaten. You want to feel energized. We have come to value the word "full" as an indicator that we have "our money's worth". If we do not feel "full" we have almost felt robbed or short-changed. A concept of resting back in your chair, after you have finished your meal and feeling full, whilst your body tries to break down the food you have eaten. If you have ever felt or experienced this - It is merely your body and gut in pain and trying to tell you something.

You want to feel light and full of energy after each meal. You should be able to eat a meal and then move straight away. You should be able to go on a brisk walk, tee it up, take a swing or even go on a run! You shouldn't feel like an old man who has just eaten a Sunday roast lunch having indulged in a bottle of red wine requiring an afternoon snooze.

It is not just food we need to question, but our choice of beverages too. I am extraordinarily slow in the mornings so naturally I would drink coffee to wake me up. Usually some seriously strong coffee too. With a morning tee time, I would find myself on the 1st green trying to make a smooth stroke for birdie and my hands were gently shaking from the caffeine and my mind was feeling anxious and analytical.

I love coffee. I love the smell, the taste, the process, and the culture. But caffeine in the morning before a round of golf was just not working. Simple solution: don't get rid of things you love - just replace it with a better option. I would challenge you to tell the difference in taste of a good decaf Americano to your normal caffeine infused rocket fuel.

No two bodies are the same. So, it is important to find what works for you and question everything. Smoking 2/3 packets a day works out to be 18,000 cigarettes a year. 15 cans of diet coke a day works out to be 515 gallons per year. With 18 professional wins and two major titles, not drinking water because he didn't like the taste and playing his best golf drunk; You could argue the case that John Daly's nutritional plan worked out just fine for him.

Takeaways...

Here are the best things I have learned along the way which have all helped with my performance on and off the golf course.

Once again, I cannot stress this enough, to be tried and tested on yourself to find what works best for you.

1. **Paleo Lifestyle** - A simple guideline: If it looks like it was made in a factory, don't eat it. If you get that feeling of being bloated after eating your current meals, what may be leading to this bloating is wheat, grains or even dairy. Paleo diet removes foods like: dairy, sugar, grains, wheat, legumes, and processed foods from your diet.

    Foods you can eat on the Paleo diet include: meat, fish, eggs, vegetables, fruits, sweet potatoes, nuts, seeds, olive and avocado oils. Wine and dark chocolate are also approved! If looking to lose excess body fat, eat proteins first, then fill up on salad after. Out of all the diet experiments I have tried, this has been the most effective and easiest to follow. Peeing on Keto strips was never fun first thing in the morning.

2. **Drop the caffeine** - One of the best things I have done in the last five years is coming off caffeine. Both on and off the course, I started to notice it was making me feel anxious and analytical. Decaf coffee is a great alternative. With 1/7th of the amount of caffeine in a cup of coffee, Chai Tea is also a good way to slowly pull yourself off the caffeine addiction if you did not want to rip off the band-aide.

3. **For on-course energy, replace carbs for fats.** I would steer away from things like flapjacks, bacon sandwiches, chocolate bars, or crisps. Basically, everything your club/pro shop sells. Instead, substitute for things like Dark chocolate 70%+, nut butter squeezes,

almonds, brazil nuts - you can even get dark chocolate coated versions of these which are superb. Biltong with the rind on is another great option. These snacks will make you feel energized, satisfied, and won't rob you of your energy levels. I would eat fruit, but only if I could not get any of the above and on the back nine/six holes. Despite natural sugars, it's still sugar.

4. **Salt and magnesium** - If you are living and playing golf somewhere hot all year round, firstly I envy you. But if you experience muscle cramps or feel like you are thirsty, make sure you add electrolytes to your water bottle. Avoid energy drinks with added electrolytes - most of them are just sugar waters. Another homemade option is just adding some salt and lemon into your water bottle.

If you have any other questions, email me at, "makingaclubchampion@gmail.com" and we can schedule a free call to create you a custom nutrition plan that will provide you with more energy and enhanced focus.

LESSON NO. 11:

HOW TO HIT MORE GREENS AND PLAY YOUR WAY INTO YOUR ROUND

There is nothing good or bad, but thinking makes it so.
—HAMLET

There are no shortcuts in the quest for perfection.
—BEN HOGAN

My dream growing up was to play on the European Tour. Testing my game in the competitive environment of College Golf in America was the next step to making this happen.

Tournaments are played over 54 holes. The first day is 36, followed by 18 holes on the final day. To win a tournament on the college golf circuit you have to shoot several under. Shooting level par is never going to cut it, even on the toughest courses.

I quickly learned that you could play your way out of a round or tournament by playing too aggressively early on. Deciding to take on pin positions that were not meant to be chased after resulted in quick bogeys, if not worse. Being several over par through the opening six to nine holes is hard to crawl back from. We played on PGA Tour venues such as PGA National (The Honda Classic) and TPC Sawgrass (The Players Championship). Courses were 7000+ yards, off the back tees with the same Sunday pin positions.

There is an art to playing your way into your game and letting the round come to you. Having the determination to win and the patience to wait for the breaks is key. To develop this skill, you must be smart about how to play your approach shots into the greens, and foster a disciplined mentality around this art. You want to be able to execute shots early on that find the safe side and the wide side of the greens. Short siding yourself and taking direct aim at a flag that was never meant to be taken on, leaving yourself 5-10ft putts, will make for a long day on the course, especially if the error is repeated.

The key to hitting more greens and building a great round is creating a discipline of aiming away from the flag for the first six holes and leaving yourself slightly longer putts for birdie but hitting greens in regulation early on.

Intentionally aiming ten yards away from the flag and executing on that shot is just the same as hitting it directly at the pin. You have just shifted the target, limiting the downside of making an unforced error and increasing your probability of a successful shot.

Making great decisions at key times will determine the outcome of your round. Great rounds are built on how good your bad shots are.

Similarities can be identified between the decision-making skills required in other professions such as a market trader or poker player. You have to assess each trade or hand of cards as a new situation. Crunch the numbers, assess what probability of success you have at that moment, and make a decision that is going to work in your favour. This game is about making calculated decisions at specific moments.

As you execute these shots early on, you will gain confidence in your shot making ability. When an opportunity presents itself, you will now be ready to take advantage of it. You will feel in control of your ball as you have been playing with discipline and slowly building confidence. When you have discipline you have freedom. You have earned respect from the course. You are cool, collected, and able to make calculated moves. You have waited patiently for these moments that favour your advantage.

As Warren Buffet, one of the world's great traders once said. "Baseball and investing go hand in hand. The great investors wait at the crease, watching ball after ball go by, until that one ball lands right in your sweet spot. Ignore the temptations. Just sit and wait for that opportunity to come to you and then when it does, take advantage of it and swing really hard."

The same is with golf. The course will stay still and always be waiting for you. While your competitors and playing partners play the ego game, acting loosely and trying to hit miraculous shots. You act cool and make decisions collectively. You plan, respect, sit, observe, and wait for the round to turn in your favour. Every time you have the urge to make an aggressive play, you go with the more conservative one until a real opportunity on the course presents itself. Then you take direct aim and pick up strokes on the course.

Jack Nicklaus would rarely kick off the tournament with a 63 or 64 but by the weekend, that is where he wanted his game to be. When we play golf, we want our confidence to grow over the course of the round or tournament week. Let the round develop and come to you, there is no need to force it. The course will give you opportunities with a short drivable par 4, a par 5 which is greenable in two, a short par 3 with no dangers surrounding the green, and a middle pin position.

Beware of the quiet golfer who plods his way around, picking up shots when everyone is dropping them. The secret to hitting more greens is to stay patient and play yourself into the round. Aim at the wide parts of the green, ignore the flags. Take your pars early on, putts can always drop for birdie.

LESSON NO. 12:

HOW TO MAKE MORE PUTTS AND GET UP AND DOWN MORE OFTEN

Just tap it in. Just tap it in. Give it a little tappy. Tap Tap Taparoo.
—HAPPY GILMORE

1. The best golfer I have ever played with...

I have been fortunate enough to have played with many great golfers both amateur and professionals all around the world, witnessing shots and rounds that could only be described as magic and make you tingle with excitement inside.

But, without doubt, a name that impressively stands out for me was a chap called Oscar Sharpe.

You may have never heard the name, however, if you are a golfer, you will know the name Butch Harmon. When seeing Oscar hit a ball growing up, he commented; "Better at 13 than Tiger Woods."

I was fortunate enough to play and compete against Oscar growing up. He was a child prodigy who was the British champion in the under-14, under-15, and under-16 age groups. In one season he won every under-16 competition he entered and became a member of the England under-18 golf team, being the youngest person ever to be selected, and beating the previous record held by Justin Rose.

He was one of those players who made impossible shots look possible. Oscar disappeared from the game, falling out of love with it and pursuing a new path. Many years later I reached out to him and asked if he would teach me, in particular his short game. Sounds like a bold statement - he had a short game that was as good as Tigers. Anyone who was lucky enough to play with him during these years would say the same thing.

I wanted to know what his mindset was when he was standing over a chip or a putt. Here are the insights and secrets from those lessons Oscar shared with me.

"When faced with any putt or shot around the green, even 100 yards and in, the secret is to keep asking yourself these two questions over and over again:

Can I see it going in?

Can I feel it going in?

Can I see it going in?

Can I feel it going in?

I would ask myself this over and over again until I got that feeling of when I could see it going in with the right speed and line. Only then I would hit the shot as I knew my mind, body and hands all believed and felt it going in,

If that is your sole focus over the ball, you will be surprised how many times you actually hole-out shots from the impossible.

Being able to silent the mind and create stillness on and around the greens to only ask this question, is crucial."

Oscar still holds the title for the youngest person to win the England title. He now lives in India teaching golf and meditation. (Ep 14 on <u>MakingAClubCampion.com</u> - Oscar Sharpe – The Story of a Child Prodigy)

2. Don't hit putts for the sake of hitting putts

The tip comes from Matt Wallace (European/ PGA Tour)

> *"Never practice hitting a putt for the sake of hitting a putt. Every time you hold the putter in your hands the mindset should be to hole it. So you are practicing and deepening the muscle of practicing quality. When you are on the practice green, hitting putts before you tee off. Unless you are standing over the ball thinking and believing you can hole it. You should not even have the putter in your hands. Every time you hold that putter, you want to have the mindset that you can hole everything you look at. So do not hit a putt without that mindset."*
> (Ep 1 on MakingAClubChampion.com - Matt Wallace – What it Takes to Win on the European Tour)

Takeaways...

When caddying on the European Tour, I noticed a common theme with players and training aides. During the week, I kept notes in the back of my yardage book, tracking which ones were the most popular.

Here are the putting training aids that some of the best players on the European Tour carry around the world with them. I hope they help take your putting to the next level.

1) **The Putting Rail**
2) **Eye mirror**
3) **Putting String**
4) **Visio Putting Matt**
5) **Visio Putting Gates**

LESSON NO.13:

THE POWER OF ROUTINES

There is nothing good or bad, but thinking makes it so.
—HAMLET

The 2003 US Masters stood out for me and Tiger didn't even win. A golfer, who many said was not long enough to win around 7,290-yard layout of The Masters, was slowly taking the course apart. Under the radar, the 344 ranked Canadian Mike Weir stated:

> "I didn't let Tiger or anybody affect what I was doing. I was so focused on my game. I'm a pretty one-dimensional player – I keep my ball in the fairway and rely on my short game. I can't unleash one 320 yards – don't have that shot. My game is not going to change because of anybody else in the field. I have to execute my game better than everybody else does."

His routine was so dialed in, Golf World reported that his pre-shot routine was mini seconds in the difference, from the time he addressed the ball to the completion of his swing.

When the pressure was on, he did not falter. Completely submerged in his own world and the things he could control, his routine made him look like he was playing a round on a summer's evening with his mates.

I was 14 at the time when Mike Weir won the masters. Inspired by what I witnessed, it showed me the power of routines. That Easter, I borrowed my mum's kitchen egg timer and took it up to the range.

After getting a rough idea of how long my routine was, I set the egg timer for 40 seconds. From visualizing and feeling the shot behind the ball to finishing the swing. This was roughly how long it was to complete my routine.

After many days and weeks living at the range, I could get my routine to a second difference on either side of 43 seconds.

This was a painful and patient practice. Not only to me but everyone on the range that also had to deal with the egg timer going off!

Ten years later, I still use the same routine for every shot. There are not many areas of the game which you are in control of. The ones which you are, do them really well.

Takeaways...

1. How to break up and simplify your routine:

Think Box - Play Box was developed by Pia Nilsson and Lynn Marriott whilst they were working with Annika Sorenstam when she was dominating the LPGA Tour.

The Think Box is the area in which you analyze the lie of the ball, the club you will use, wind direction, the type of shot you want to play. You survey the landscape and take note of where the trees, lakes, or sand traps are. You calculate the yardage and where you want to leave the ball on the fairway or green. This is where you prepare and gather as much data as possible to give yourself the best chance of executing the shot.

Once you feel comfortable that you have gathered all the information with the shot at hand, take a step across the decision line and into the Play Box. When you cross this imaginary line, you should stop thinking anything technical and just play!

There must be a total commitment to the shot when you are in the Play Box. If you get over the ball and you are not feeling comfortable or still thinking technical swing thoughts, back off, retreat to the Think Box, start your routine again. The only time when there is any indecision should be when you are in the Think Box.

In the Play Box, there is no thought. You have done the work, you have performed the mental rehearsal. It is time to just let go and let your body do the work. This is where you operate in the present moment.

For more on this, visit (Ep 31: Pia Nilsson – How To Birdie Every Hole) and (Ep 32: Lynn Marriott – Mental Game Golf Tips – What to Think When Over the Golf Ball on <u>MakingAClubChampion.com</u>)

2. Find your routine

A routine is like a putting stroke, it has to be personal to you. The most important element would be the speed and rhythm of your routine. Experiment and find what that is for you.

3. The Egg Timer

A good way to start getting clear with your routine is to write down all the moving steps in your journal. This could look like the following.

- One tap of the club on the floor
- Choose a target and where I want the ball to finish
- Feel the club in your hands to target
- Visualize ball flight
- One practice swing
- Move into the golf ball
- Two taps with club on floor

- Look at target
- Look at ball
- Hit.

Once you have all the moving parts, get yourself a countdown timer or stopwatch and dial in your routine to Mike Weir's precision.

LESSON NO. 14:

HOW TO DEVELOP MENTAL TOUGHNESS

Why would I pay for a physiologist to tell me how good I am.
—IAN POULTER

To be like the rock that the waves keep crashing over. It stands unmoved
and the rage of the sea falls still around it.
—MARCUS AURELIUS

Anyone who isn't embarrassed of who they were last year probably isn't
learning enough.
—ALAIN DE BOTTON

What's this about you breaking a rake and throwing it in the woods? I didn't
break it, I was merely testing its durability, and I *placed* it in the woods
cause it's made of wood and I thought he should be with his family.
—VIRGINIA & HAPPY GILMORE

A person's success in life can usually be measured by the number of
uncomfortable conversations he or she is willing to have.
—TIM FERRISS

Every golfer knows the real challenge, the real battle is not between you and
the opponent or you and the course. It is between you and yourself.
—SAM JARMAN

How could he hit it that bad and be nearly tied for the lead? I had been watching Ian Poulter warm up on the range at the Wentworth PGA earlier that morning and he could barely find it.

Pulls, hooks and slices. He had all of it covered except the middle of the range.

What us golfers call the double miss. A.k.a., "what the f*** is going on?"

I was so horrified by what I saw, I took out my phone and went online seeking a betting agency to establish if there were any odds on players to miss the cut or finish dead last.

I scrolled through my phone viewing the online betting options that came up, one of them was - Ian Poulter to beat Lee Westwood at evens. The opportunity immediately caught my attention.

As I looked up to see if Poults was still carving more balls into the side netting, Lee Westwood entered the range. All my focus was on him now. I had to see what kind of form Westwood was in, for me to take advantage of this opportunity.

If he was hitting it just as bad as Poulter, there was no bet, but this was Westwood. One of the most consistent ball strikers on the European Tour.

As he walked slowly down the range to find a flat lie to hit off, he found a spot right next to Ian Poulter. I now had them both warming up directly in front of me, no more than 20 ft away.

Time was disappearing expeditiously. I knew the odds were not going to be up much longer as they were both teeing off in no less than an hour. So I had about 50 or so balls to make that "decision."

Lee picked out his wedge and started his routine with some small 10-yard chips, then working up to 20/30, and 40/50 yard shots.

As his body warmed up, he then started to hit some at the 100-yard Titleist range marker. The first ball hit the sign. The second ball hit the sign and the third ball missed by a foot.

I started to enter the number £1000 next to the odds on the app and it was showing a return of £1980, a £980 profit. I am not a gambler, but this just felt too good to be true.

"Hold up Christopher", I said.

"Remember to stay patient, any tour pro can hit a wedge to a target".

Meanwhile, Poults was continually finding the left net with his driver and seemed to be in a whirlwind of emotions getting frustrated that he was hitting it more like a 20 handicapper than a world-beater. It got so bad, he started to bring out some practice aids, alignment rods and what appeared to be a floating pipe from a swimming pool?!

Focus went back to Westwood, "just bring out a longer club, and I will place this bet immediately."

He reached for his bag, which appeared to be an 8/9 iron and changed his target once again with some gentle swings to the 150 markers.

First one hit it, second one missed by three yards and third one landed just short of it.

The ball was not moving in the air. Just knuckleball after knuckleball.

I wasn't the only one on the range in awe of this ball-striking performance, the fellow spectators around me were all in silence listening to the balls ricocheting off the yardage markers. It was magical to watch.

I was still holding out though. The shorter clubs are easy for anyone to look somewhat impressive. As soon as I saw a long iron or wood in Westwoods hands I was going to go all in. With only 20 mins left until they were due on the first tee, the fear of missing out on this prosperous opportunity was looming on my mind.

I was fortunate enough to witness this precision ball-striking performance before from Westwood, roughly five years ago, at the World Matchplay at TPC Harding Park in San Francisco.

That time he was on the far-left side of the range and in the distance was a leafy tree branch sticking out around 150 yards. Ball after ball was brushing the edge or missing just a few yards to the right each time, never touching or whacking into the branch or the tree, just these pure baby cuts sliding past it and kissing the last couple of leaves. Shot after shot, executed to perfection.

Finally, Westwood had pulled out a long iron.

I informed myself that if he hit any of these shots as pure as the last ones, the bet was being placed. Westwood has always been a great driver of the ball; I will hold out on his reputation.

He pulled the club away effortlessly. The ball took off and simmered over the 200-yard marker with a gentle one to two-yard fade. After a couple more knuckleballs landing around the 200-yard marker, I felt I had enough confidence in what I had experienced during the last 45 mins or so to make the bet.

As an investor on the golf course once told me "you can only make a decision with the information you have at the time." I was all in.

I punched £1000 onto the online betting app - placing all on Westwood to beat Poults in a straight head-to-head match. With a confirmation notification, "your bet has been placed", it was on!

I then imagined scenes of Westwood moving to his woods and carving them over the right side of the range netting. But he didn't, Westwood continued to move through his bag, hitting knuckleball after knuckleball.

As they finished up the last couple of shots, their caddies prepared their bags to walk to the first tee. The nerves started to kick in. The bet was placed, there was not much I could do now. They were not paired in the same group. So, I decided to follow Poulter for the first nine as he was teeing off first, then drop back and watch Westwood on the back nine.

I managed to find a spot in between the crowd to watch Poults tee off. After a roaring round of applause, being a favorite amongst the golfing fans, Poults stood up on the first tee and pumped one, splitting the first fairway 320 yards straight down the middle.

"You have got to be kidding me! Where the hell did that from!?"

I followed Poults through that front nine and, needless to say, it was a masterclass display.

Shot after shot, executed with patience and precision. Always hitting it to the wider part of the fairways and attacking pins when he saw an opportunity to go for it.

Gambling and golf almost have this poetic symmetry. Knowing when to play safe and hit it to the wider part of the green, knowing when to attack and take risks to go after a pin and chase after a birdie. It is a game of mental decisions and executing upon them at key points during the round.

Somehow Poults had full control of his ball on the course. Moments ago, I would have bet a 20 handicapper beating him. Now he was right up there on the leaderboard! He made the turn, bogey-free, shooting three-under par.

I had seen enough, and so had my palpitations. I moved back a couple of holes to find Westwood who was plodding along at level par.

Westwood's driver was on a piece of string. His driving never got him into trouble. He was masterful at creating beautiful angles on the course. He could hit it down certain parts of the fairway to open up holes and hit the ball under the hole. What often let his game down was his short game and putting, with putts consistently shaving the hole, but never quite going in.

With the two par 5's to finish at Wentworth, I pulled out my phone and refreshed the screen to see how Poults had finished. With a bogey on the par-five 17th and a par down the 18th he finished two under for the day.

If Westwood could get on a bit of a run, the bet was very much on. My body moved from somewhat of a nervous state, to an awakened excitement.

Westwood had picked up a shot on the par-four 15th and birdied 17, getting up and down from just off the green and was walking to the 18th tied with Poults at two-under.

I buried my way through the fans on the 18th tee, to get a view of Westwood. He had walked over to the bag and pulled out his 3 wood. Once again, he pipped a soft buttery cut that split the middle of the fairway.

In prime position, Westwood went for the green in two, the ball took off right at the flag and didn't move, landed safely over the water just 20 feet from the hole, hitting the green in two on par 5.

A roar of claps echoed around the grandstand behind the 18th green.

I couldn't bear to watch in case he somehow three-putted, so I waited in the tented village. A red block finally came up on the scoreboard, shooting a -3 to Poulters -2 under. The funds automatically showed up into my account, euphoric and trembling at the same time I went straight into the bar and celebrated with a couple of gin & tonics.

After the initial excitement wore off, I went to sit in the grandstand on the 18th to watch the last couple of groups come in and reflect on the day.

As I sat there calming down from the adrenaline-fueled four to five hours, one question kept coming up:

"How could someone hit it that bad on the range in a warm-up, yet strike it so well when it mattered?"

There was much to learn about this experience I thought.

Although Westwood's ball-striking was awe-inspiring because of how tight his misses were, there was something about Poults that most golfers could all relate to and learn from.

I quickly concluded that whatever Ian Poulter was telling himself, (that internal dialogue) from the range, onto that first tee, must have been extremely strong and compelling.

He couldn't have been thinking about the entire bucket of balls he missed on the range. His mindset and the internal story almost would have been the opposite from what I had just experienced. It was like he somehow arrived with the confidence of Westwood's warm-up on the first tee!

I remember this experience striking me so profoundly. It was a summer where I noticed what was going on outside of the game was being reflected in my game. When I was out on the course, I didn't aim for any specific target. I stood up on the tee and swung away and wished upon a prayer. The ball could go anywhere, often ending up in vague and unknown places on the course.

Once where I could stand on any tee box with confidence aiming down the left and hit a buttery cut, I would stand on the first and pray that I would find it again.

My short game was keeping me in the game, yet I was relying so much on this part of my game, the pressure chamber broke and I developed the yips in my chipping and putting.

Something so creative and free started to become mechanical and technical. Where I once would see and create different flights, landing points, spin and the ball vanishing into the hole from all angles, I now felt stuck, rigid, and stubborn.

Witnessing that performance from Ian Poulter told me bluntly, I can figure this out. It is mind over matter and your thoughts do not own you, but you can control your thoughts and the internal input and story you tell yourself.

You can become aware of what you are thinking, do something about it and if I was totally honest with myself and started to make hard choices, there was an opportunity to turn this around.

With golf being a game so close to my heart, I thought the best place to sort this out was to take a very close look at the specific words and language I was using during my rounds.

With the English summer evenings staying light until around 9:30/10:00 pm. I felt a little spring in my step. Excited and full of inspiration, I dashed to the Berkshire Golf Club, a beautiful heathland golf club just minutes away from Wentworth.

I felt like that kid again, just get me on those fairways. I was excited about driving there and just wanted to get out onto that first tee box and swing the club. Poulter's mindset and attitude inspired me and I started to believe that I could make a big change in my life and on the golf course.

From working as an assistant pro at Leighton Buzzard golf course, giving lessons to youngsters at £1 per lesson to ranking number five in the world at one point, Poulter was a great example of how someone could turn their life around.

Arriving at an empty car park, walking down the first with the entire course to myself I thought, "if I said out loud exactly what I was thinking, it would make vivid and clear what my internal dialogue was when I was over the ball."

The first couple of holes were interesting. Here is what came up:

1st Hole - Par 5 - 1st shot

"Trouble on the right"
"Hazard, red stake on the left"

"Huge tree on the left, won't be able to hit over that"
"Thick heather both left and right,"
"Just find the fairway"
"Can't afford to hit it into the heather, do not find the heather!"

2nd Hole: Par 3

"Hate this hole"
"Always find the right trap, do not hit in there"
"Take the par and run"

From an outsider in, you would see a golfer standing on the tee box with a pretty tidy swing. But the internal dialogue was another story. It was of a golfer that had never played before with little confidence.

We think somewhere between 60,000 to 70,000 thoughts in one day. Thoughts and the words we use are so powerful that if repeated often enough, become unconscious thinking. When thinking in such a detrimental way with some of the words and phrases illustrated, I was merely just living what I was thinking.

Was Ian Poulter thinking like this? Hell f***ing no, I thought.

Okay then, what would he be thinking? What would Ian Poulter be saying to himself?

I asked the question again:

"If I took a step into Ian Poulter's head, what are the exact words he would be saying to himself"?

I closed my eyes in the middle of the fairway and just stopped and paused for a moment. I imagined myself stepping into Ian Poulter's mind as he was walking to the first hole at Wentworth earlier that morning.

"Stripe a soft fade at that tree in the middle of the fairway"
"That will leave us the best angle to attack the pin,"

"I can hit that shot all day long"
"I want the whole world to watch me hit this shot,"
"Confident swing, you got this"
Something like that, I reckon.

If we can hold onto an idea, we begin to wire and shape our brain around that idea. Even if I was not hitting it like that, what a powerful place to operate from.

I started to explore and look deeper within.

Perhaps it is just not over the ball. Where was my mind in between the shots?

Walking down the fairway, I would say all what I was thinking out loud.

If anyone was around me, they would have most likely questioned my sanity.

What would he be saying to himself in-between shots I thought?
"Life is great"
"What a beautiful moment this is, and how lucky am I to be out here playing here doing something I love"
"I am so grateful to be playing this game."
"Just tell me where you want this, and I will hit it there"
Something along those lines, I reckon.

But how can you start the change if you are not feeling and experiencing any of these? I started to realize that the best way to predict your future is to create it not from the known, but from the unknown.

Me and my game were so far away from any of those ideas and thoughts, they were very much an unknown foreign place. But if I was ever going to move into an empowering state, the unknown was the only place and first destination I had to go. I couldn't create a new future or a better me, by holding onto the emotions of the past. The best way to predict my future was merely to create it from the unknown.

As I started to recite those phrases over and over again in my mind, my body language started to change, my shoulders were back, chin up, I started to walk with a bit of confidence.

Even if I did hit a stray shot, I wasn't attached to it. Similar to life, golf is not always going to be perfect. You are going to make mistakes, you are going to make the wrong decisions but that is okay. If you make a mistake or miss a shot, you will learn from it and have the next shot covered.

Over and over and over again, I was brainwashing myself through the power of the words.

And it was working...

Nine holes later, I had just played some of the most flawless golf. It was a different game I had been playing for the previous six months. I quickly learned the power of the internal dialogue and that whatever you focus on, you will feel.

This is when I understood what mental strength was. When you are at your lowest, but you are still fighting and grinding like hell to get better.

Takeaways...

How do you talk to yourself during your round? What are the questions you ask of yourself?

Do you beat yourself up, play with fear and question why you play this game? If so, these thoughts will manifest themselves in your reality.

You are not the story you tell yourself, but stories are powerful enough to take over and define who you are.

Epicurus was a radical ancient Greek philosopher. He taught his students the art of living a simple, ascetic life, and living in moderation; believing that by limiting oneself to just a few natural desires (friendship, simple food, water etc.), one could lead a happy life.

He gave his followers aphorisms which would spring easily to mind when most needed, such as "He who is not satisfied with a little, is satisfied with nothing".

Slogans can help deal with adversity or disturbance without recourse to detailed thought or study. Some stories can be empowering, and some can be deflating and detrimental.

Eldrick Woods embodies a powerful animal at the top of the food chain, the "Tiger." Commentators would say, "he's got that look in his eye." "Watch out, Tiger is about". The red shirt on a Sunday. The colour of power and victory. The colour of blood. The colour when you beat your opponents in battle. Competitors most likely lost tournaments down the stretch because of the story that "Tiger" stood for. The story that Tiger was told growing up by his father.

When we introduce powerful slogans and empowering stories. We can change our identity for the better. We start to play the role of something bigger and more powerful.

These slogans and stories can also be detrimental to us:

- "I always hit it right on that hole"
- "I never hit a good shot on this hole"
- "I always hit it on the water here"
- "Why do I always get that bounce"
- "My putts never go in"

They can also be the most powerful:

- "I always hit a good shot on this hole"
- "I never miss a putt inside 3 feet"
- "When the going gets tough, I get going"

- "I knew that put was going in, even before I hit it, it just felt right"
- "Never, never, never give up". Winston Churchill
- "The more I practice, the luckier I get". Gary Player

Golfers are riddled with superstitions and associations with luck. From always having to mark their ball in a certain way, to wearing the same shirt or socks in a competition.

Superstition is a mistaken feeling that we think we can control fate. We have built-in associations with events like "if I walk under that ladder, I will get bad luck." "If I break a mirror, I will sin for seven years."

I have thrown salt over my left shoulder for as long as I can remember because my mum told me as a child that if I spilled salt and didn't throw it over my shoulder, I would be unlucky.

The internal dialogue is "the universe will conspire to work in my favour if these events happen to us." We start to build associations between random events and experiences that have happened to us in the wider world. We draw a cause and effect when there simply aren't any.

Turn any obstacles you have into triumphs. Discover and get clear on the story you are telling yourself. Decide if you are going to choose an empowering story or a destructive one. It's your choice.

LESSON NO. 15:

HOW TO BECOME A MASTER FROM 125 YARDS AND IN

There isn't enough daylight in any one day to practice all the shots you need to.

You're gonna need a blanket and suntan lotion, cause you're never gonna get off that beach, just like the way you never got into the NHL, ya JACKASS.
—JEERING FAN

I had just finished my second year playing college golf in America and needed to work on my game. Heading back home to England for the summer, I asked my coach what the biggest difference I could make in my game is.

"Your short game has to be great to compete at the college level. To attempt to make it on PGA/ European Tour it has to be electrifying."

With this in mind, I wasted no time and started going to the range every day with my three wedges (48, 54 and 60). After nearly a week's worth of practice hitting 200 balls a day, my hands started to develop painful calluses. It was clear that rep practice alone was not going to award me with an electrifying short game, I needed instant recognition that when I was over a shot on the course, I knew exactly what to do.

More often than not, the key to success and solving your problems, whether they be on or off the golf course, is to ask better questions.

What were the drills and systems I could implement to give my short game the best results?

The answer was to have complete control of my yardages. To get that result, the best method I researched was going to create a clock-like system to tighten up my distances and yardage control.

I wanted such confidence that any distance from 125 yards and in, I knew I could Bushnell the flag, and know that it was 110 yards with a 52 degree at 10 o'clock swing to give myself the very best chance to get the ball up and down.

That summer I spent it with my shag bag and my 4 wedges. Rehearsing swings at different positions on my body. My three positions were at 10, 11 and 12 o'clock (some like chest, shoulders, and head).

From once where I just had three shots in my bag, I now had 12 different shots from 125 yards and in. Pretty much any yardage I was given, I knew I could stand over the ball and know what club I needed and what specific position. This would allow me to hit my numbers and fire at the flags with confidence. This became a deadly strength to my game.

It takes hundreds of hours to get this perfect this drill. Do not underestimate the dedication behind developing and implementing this method into your game.

If there was any secret to mastering 125 yards and in, it was this system and many hours of hard work.

Takeaways...

1. If you carry three wedges, get yourself a fourth and either drop a long iron or wood. The set up I would recommend is as follows;
    *   Pitching Wedge = 48 degrees.

- Gap Wedge = 52 degrees
- Sand Wedge = 56 degrees
- Lob Wedge = 60 degrees.

2. When it comes to building the positions in your swing, start off with putting in the reps with just one position and one club, e.g.,10 o'clock with 48 degrees. Once you feel comfortable, work out the average yardage of where the ball lands, then move up to the next position with the same club, 11 o'clock with 48 degrees and so on.

3. Two quotes to consider from Dave Alred, coach to Luke Donald and Francesco Molinari:

"You look like a pretty good golfer to me, doesn't mean diddly squat frankly. But if you know, you can hit 10 shots with a 54-degree wedge and 5 of those will be within 10ft of the pin and the others will be within 15ft of the pin. Now that is a fact. You have achieved that. How can I get that even better? I can get more shots within 10ft and so on,

Keep track of all of the previous practice data, and try to beat your previous best. You now have facts that actually can prove you can do it. And therefore when you went into a tournament, there was a factual basis behind your approach and it gave you a lot more confidence.

If you're going to practice you need to practice against num-bers, otherwise you do not know if you are getting any better. So, whether it is nearer to the pin or consistently. There will be numbers to show it. And the biggest thing about confidence is. Confidence should be based on fact - i.e., you have already done it before." (Ep 12 on MakingAClubChampion.com —DAVE ALRED – The Pressure Principles.)

4. Having all 12 shots and yardages stored in your head is far too much information to be carrying around when playing. I was fortunate enough to play at the same club as Chris Wood growing up (3 European Tour wins, 1 x Ryder Cup). One afternoon I was paired with Chris in a County match. He shared with me his secret on how he would write the three positions/yardages on the back of his shafts with each wedge. I have also seen players write them down on the size of a business card, laminate it, and keep it in with their scorecard.

5. No one said this game was easy. If you want results, turn up and put in the hours.

LESSON NO. 16:

HOW TO LET GO OF YOUR GOLFING DEMONS AND STAY PRESENT ON THE GOLF COURSE

I play with friends, but we don't play friendly games.
—BEN HOGAN

The man who says he is, and the man who says he isn't…both are correct.
—CONFUCIUS

Lot of pressure. You've gotta rise above it. You've got to harness in the good energy, block out the bad. Harness... energy... block... bad. Feel the flow, feel it. It's circular. Its like a carousel-- you pay the quarter, you get on the horse. It goes up and down and around. Circular... circle. With the music, the flow. All good things.
—POTTER, HAPPY GILMORE

I'm trying to free your mind, Neo. But I can only show you the door. You're the one that has to walk through it.
—MORPHEUS, THE MATRIX

We cannot create a new future, by holding on to the emotions of the past.
—DR JOE DISPENZA

I always told myself I was never good enough.

This story motivated me to practice and work harder at my game, but more often than not, it was detrimental to my performance.

Sometimes my dad would say to me "you lost the tournament before you even showed up."

Small things would throw me off guard. From what the other players could shoot before I even teed it up and how they handled themself walking around the putting green, what they played off to how far they hit it. The course, its length, seeing tough pin positions driving in and even to the weather!

Golf can be a lonely and insular game. You really have to go out there and play for yourself. If you are trying to impress or beat others, you are playing the wrong game. The real battle is between you and the course.

Two thousand years ago, a Roman slave called Epictetus, a prominent figure in the ancient school of Stoic philosophy, gave voice to the notion: "What upsets people is not things themselves but their judgments about these things." In other words, it is not events that cause our problems but rather our reactions to them: the stories we tell ourselves.

There are only two things we can control - our thoughts and our actions. Everything else falls on the other side of the line: the things we can't control.

We tend to spend time and energy worrying about things we can't control. Instead, a better approach is to simply decide that everything outside our control is absolutely fine as it is and leave it at that.

We go through life owned by the stories we tell ourselves which are often historic and charged narratives - things we've learned since childhood that we don't even consciously realize are still affecting our attitude and performance. We carry these negative stories around with us, like a suitcase full of bricks, they can have power over us if we allow them to.

"If you are pained by external things, it is not that they disturb you, but your own judgment of them. And it is in your power to wipe out that judgment now" (Marcus Aurelius, private journals).

One summer, I read a book about Ben Hogan and how he would keep his head down when arriving at the range and take himself to the last spot on the far right-hand side. If he looked up, he would see no one. Faldo would ignore his playing partners, keep his head down and go about his own business.

Whatever your golfing demons are, it is important to realize that it is not what we see or experience that causes our internal battles, but rather our reactions to those events and the stories we tell ourselves.

Therefore, if we find ourselves feeling negative emotions (fear, intimidation, anxiety, sadness, etc.), we can realize that our emotions stem from within. We can decide to let them go.

Takeaways...

A fit body and a calm mind, must be earned and constantly worked on and never bought.

—NAVAL RAVIKANT

I'm going to give you a little advice. There's a force in the universe that makes things happen. And all you have to do is get in touch with it, stop thinking, let things happen, and be the ball.

—TY WEBB

'Everyone you meet is fighting a battle you know nothing about. Be kind. Always.'

—BRAD MELTZER

Life is suffering. Suffering is caused by cravings and attachments. Find the route cause of the cravings, attachments and you will discover nirvana, which is heaven.
—MALCOLM LEWIS

Here is a list of other activities outside of golf, which help with deepening the muscles of awareness and presence.

- Rock climbing
- Waking up without checking your phone
- Meditation
- Journaling/Writing
- Service work in helping others
- Drawing/painting/sketching
- Building a wall, build a fence
- Read a book
- Gardening
- Star gazing
- Sit down in silence and do nothing, just listen to your thoughts and what surfaces
- Pay it forward, buy cup of coffee and one more for the stranger behind you
- Cleaning. Clean your house, clean your car, clean your clubs?
- Removing/donating: Wardrobe is a great place to start
- Slacklining

All self-help advice filters down to "choose long-term over short-term."

Out of all the above, just sitting down with your thoughts in silence for 10 mins a day is the scariest yet most powerful. To measure the quality of your life, simply do nothing, see how it feels. The quality of your mind is the quality of your life and game.

Another suggestion worth trying is slacklining. As soon as you are not present/still with your thoughts you will fall off. (*Man on Wire* is a great documentary on this). You're probably thinking this has nothing to do with golf, what a waste of time this will be, but practicing some of the above skill sets will spill over into your game. The most testing task for the golfer is to get out of their own way.

LESSON NO. 17:

HOW TO SWING THE CLUB FASTER AND HIT FURTHER

It is not because things are difficult that we do not dare, it is because we do not dare that things are difficult.

—SENECA

It was the second hole and my teammate's ball flew 50 yards over mine before the bounce.

Welcome to college golf, I thought...

Having been personally taught by Hank Haney, who had a swing that resembled Tiger Woods in 2007. He was 6ft 2, lean, mean, had a clubhead speed of 120+ mph.

The ball left the clubface like a firework as it was sent into the stratosphere.

On the other hand, my game was quite different.

5ft 7 on a good day, swing speed of 105 - 110mph, with a squeezed-out fade that left the clubface like a warm fart and would tickle its way hopefully down the fairway at 260-270 yards off the tee, if I swung out of my shoes and stepped on one with a howling wind, I could get it out to 280-290.

Our team was made up of 15 guys with five spots each week to play in the tournaments. Getting a spot on the team for any given week a privilege. There would usually be four qualifying rounds. The top three lowest gross scores would automatically qualify and then there would be the coach's picks.

College tournaments were set up like PGA Tour tournaments, playing off the same tees and pin positions as the pros.

We were treated like PGA Tour Pros. Everything was paid for, accommodation, ranges balls, three rounds of golf to banquet dinners. The only difference was no million-dollar prize money or the fans. The occasional mum and dad walking around the course cheering on from the buggy path.

When I arrived in North Carolina for my first season as a college golfer, my coach made me aware of my limitations.

Our club, where most of our qualifying rounds took place, was a classic North Carolina course designed by Donald Ross, called Myers Park Country Club. You had to be long off the tee and be precise with your shots into the green. Greens ran from front to back, leaving the ball short of the green and below the hole was a priority. Otherwise, it was like putting a marble down a granite work surface.

The second hole was a 450-yard par four. A good drive down the right would leave you with a flat lie for your approach. With my teammate just piping one down the middle all of 320 yards into a warm, gentle Carolina wind.

I stood up next, aimed down the right to hit a big draw off the tree line to get every bit out of the drive and get it down the fairway. With a fade being my natural shot shape, I always struggled to move the ball right to left. This time the ball slung down the right with a 15-yard draw on it.

Walking down the fairway with a slight Rory McIlroy bounce in my stride, I walked to the brow of the hill and I could see two balls glistening in the Carolina sunshine. However, there was a good 50/60 yards difference between them.

"How could that be?!"

I took out my Bushnell and had 207 left to the pin in.

Standing next to my bag, my coach asked me what I was going to hit in. I answered,

"I could possibly step on a 3 iron coach, but I think with this wind - it's a soft hybrid with a touch of fade"

I waited to see his eyes roll, but with no judgment I got a military-like order response back:

"Let's see it"

I struck the ball cleanly and the ball took off heading right at the pin.

"Be right" I ordered.

The ball was tracking right at it but came up 10 yards short of the green.

"I have just hit a full driver and full hybrid and I am still short! What is going on!?"

My teammate walked to his ball, like coming out of a supermarket and trying to find his car somewhere in the abyss.

Coach asked the same question to my teammate:

"What's your number?"

"142."

I pretended I didn't hear that number and that I wasn't remotely interested in the game he was playing - but It was quite the opposite. I took a deep interest in every word.

"Going straight at it, coach, it's a sand wedge - not much shape - just left if anything."

It was said with such clarity, objectivity, and ease, as though nothing else mattered. It was as though he was saying, "this is what I am going to do, this is how it is going to be. If it doesn't happen this way, then who cares?"

"Let's see it."

Overhearing this conversation, took a couple of inches off that 5ft 7 to a more Bilbo Baggins sort of height.

"Sand wedge!! What! How!? What planet did he come from! What mutants am I up against?!"

"I've just ripped my best drive, stood on a hybrid, and barely made it to the front of the green!"

He stood over his ball, with a smooth flick of the hands and a 3/4 backswing. The ball took on a direct line at the flag with no shot shape and landed on the safe side of the green, just 10ft away from the hole.

I tried to not let it affect me, but I was in awe of his style of play. If they both looked back at me, I would have been green with envy.

The likes of Luke Donald were going to be squeezed out of the field. I could see golf transitioning into a game of raw untapped power. Physiques and frames like Bryson Dechambeau, Brooks Koepka and with the flexibility of Camilo Vijegas were going to be dominant forces moving forward. Most college coaches now recruit on athletic ability, some of the first questions they now ask are: *"How tall are you and what's your weight"?*

I was now competing against the very best in America who had advantageous genetic qualities. Bombing it over 300 yards consistently, they didn't place the ball around the course. They stood up on tee shots and took lines over corners and trees which I just didn't see and hit it with no fear. Launching it down the fairway as far as they could, flicking a wedge onto the green and then going again. The game was being played by a different type of athlete and the old school fashion way of positioning your ball around the course was getting left behind. "Bomb and gauge" was the new mentality.

These tall, powerful, and strong athletes that once decided to dedicate their lives to Baseball, Basketball, American Football, and Lacrosse were now shifting over into golf. I always thought if you could take a player who had the athletic ability that could generate serious clubhead speed, and taught them course management, a winning mindset, and a deadly short game, you would have a player makeup to destroy golf courses.

Later that evening, coach asked me to come to his office and talk about my game.

Although I shot a good number and put myself in contention for a spot on the team - I felt a part of me had been crushed out there.

Was I built for this new age game? Did I have the power game to compete and win on a 7000+ yard tour venue course?

"The game is all about dispersion son...

The longer you have in, the less likely you are going to hit it straight. We need to get you hitting it further throughout your bag, that way you will be coming in with shorter irons and wedges. This is a deadly weapon and approach to the game I am looking for."

My head and heart sank. I knew he wasn't impressed with my game. I knew I wasn't what he was looking for.

He went on:

"The average dispersion of 10 balls with wedges is going to be a lot tighter than a player who is coming in with mid-irons. The courses we will be playing, you are going to be hitting into greens from too far back. You have a great game, but to make it on tour, or for you to have any chance to win, we need to get your speed up, big time."

I couldn't disagree with him - it made perfect sense.

I knew there were smaller players on tour that pounded it out there. The previous summer, I remember having my picture taken next to Rory Mcilroy at Wentworth for the BMW Championship - we were the same frame and size, and he was one of the longest hitters on tour. So, I knew my height or weight wasn't the main barrier.

Over the last seven years, I have tried all sorts of training techniques to help increase my swing speed.

Here are the lessons learned and secrets for increasing your swing speed and hitting the ball further.

1. Plyometrics

In golf, you want explosive movements. There is no better workout I have done for this than plyometrics. Plyometrics ("plyo," for short) used to be called "jump training." It is a style of training that uses speed and force of different movements to build muscle power. With combination of pushups, throwing, running, jumping, kicking, it covers all muscle groups from core, arms, legs, glutes and back.

If you are looking to do anything with more speed and intensity, Plyometrics does that and more.

There are dozens of classes on YouTube for free to get you started.

2. How to Build Your Own Home Gym for Under $100

If you look at any power hitter on tour, they all have a strong base from where they hit from. Consider John Rham, Jason Day, and Hideki Matsuyama, just to name a few. They have legs built like tree trunks and strong wide v-shaped lats to pull the club down from. When I first started to work out with golf in mind, I focused solely on these muscle groups. After three months of training, I had put on 10lbs of muscle and went back to the college trainer for a check-in.

His first words when he saw me..

"what happened to your core?"

I had worked endlessly on the big muscles but forgot about my mid-section.

"The core is your bike frame, it holds everything together. Without that you have no frame, you have nothing. Get back to work."

So, the big three muscle groups to work on are legs, back, and core.

You may see results quickly from training legs and back but be patient with your core. It takes time.

When it comes to training, keep things simple and keep showing up. (Revisit no. 8 for more on this.)

For example, having a kettlebell around the house, I find far more effective than a gym membership. It reduces the barrier of having to get in your car and making the journey to the gym. When the queue/trigger is right there in front of you, all you have to do is pick it up and you're on your way.

So to build your own home gym for under $100 for explosive power and speed. I would recommend the following:

a) KettleBell
b) Pull up bar
c) Yoga matt
d) Perfect Pushups

That is all you need to build a great golfing physique and feel strong over the ball.

For specific exercises and routines of how to use these in the most effective way. Feel free to email me at <u>makingaclubchampion@gmail.com</u> and I can advise and build you a specific weekly workout program for your health and your game.

3. Range of motions

When you add strength, the most important thing not to forget is to add range of motion along the way. After that story with my coach, I went out and trained to get stronger and bulk up. My ego wanted to prove him wrong. Net result, I actually started to hit it shorter. One of the biggest mistakes I made when trying to get stronger and quicker, was to forget all about stretching.

When you lift the weight and build strength you are contracting and shortening the muscle. So, you need to be doing the opposite and elongating them along the way. I have never particularly enjoyed stretching/conditioning - but here are the best bits I have found to make it fun and effective.

a) *Myofascial ball* - A small ball the size of a lacrosse ball, that is specifically designed for use on any area of the body. It is a simple but effective tool for applying just the right amount of pressure to fascia, muscles, and trigger points to ease myofascial restrictions, tightness, and muscle spasm, as well as relieving pain. Comparable to a masseuse wherever you travel.

b) *Resistant Gym bands* - These are great to leave lying around in your bedroom. What looks like a tire cable, these rubber tubed bands are great to open your hamstrings and work out your hip flexors.

c) *Pulse roll* - A vibrating peanut ball for myofascial release, trigger point therapy, deep tissue massage. It can be used on almost any part of the body but works wonders on the glutes and calves specifically. It does all the hard work for you.

d) ***Rumble roller*** - Painful, but brilliant. If you have some particularly tight muscles this is the one that will release final knots and sore points. Great for lats, IT bands and calves.

e) ***Speed sticks*** - This was one tool that I could not help to notice in Tour Players bags when caddying. They carried these with them to the gym, on the range and back at the hotel room. A slightly heavier weighted looking club with a weight on the end. That encourages you to build up a quicker swing.

LESSON NO. 18:

HOW TO FIND YOUR GAME AND CHOOSE THE LONG-TERM PATH TO MASTERY

The first principle is that you must not fool yourself — and you are the easiest person to fool.
—RICHARD FEYNMAN

It's hard to dance with the devil on your back.
—HEARD ON THE RADIO

Yeah, to the gods. That he is fallible. That perfection is unattainable. And now the weight begins shifting back to the left, pulled by the powers inside the earth. It's alive, this swing! A living sculpture and down through contact, always down, striking the ball crisply, with character. A tuning fork goes off in your heart and your balls. Such a pure feeling is the well-struck golf shot. Now the follow through to finish. Always online. The reverse C of the Golden Bear!
—ROY MCAVOY

Yep…Inside each and every one of us is one true authentic swing… Somethin' we was born with… Somethin' that's ours and ours alone… Somethin' that can't be taught to ya or learned… Somethin' that got to be remembered… Over time the world can, rob us of that swing… It get buried inside us under all our wouldas and couldas and shouldas.
—BAGGER VANCE

The sculpture is already complete within the marble block, before I start my work. It is already there, I just have to chisel away the superfluous material.
—MICHELANGELO

It was past midnight and I had been watching hours upon hours of YouTube videos of Danny Willet.

Not your normal behaviour of a 21 year-old on a Saturday evening.

Practicing in front of the mirror in my dorm room, I stood imagining I was him, trying to replicate his transition and take away with his driver.

The next week it would be the Rory Mcilroy shoulder turn. And then the upright putting position of Steve Stricker.

I loved how Luke Donald kept his hands quiet through the ball and hit his wedge shots with his core.

I would walk down the fairways, imagining I was Retief Goosen replicating his calm, poised temperament.

On the first tee, I would stand behind the ball and go through my routine with the same discipline as if I were Mike Weir.

I would steal and pinch the best from each player and mash it all together to make it my own.

I thought this was a strategy for success, but it only pulled me further away from who I was.

Over the course of time, I was just getting more and more lost and further away from connecting to my authentic swing and self on the golf course.

I forgot how to be me and play my own game.

We can look within by going back to our earliest memories as a child.

During these early years, we can recall the signs of our unique traits and qualities that make us our authentic selves.

We cannot rationally explain why we are so drawn to certain things, objects, words, sounds, or activities when we are young. We are naturally pulled to them from within. As we get older, we often lose contact with these natural inclinations.

We stop listening from within and instead listen to masters or other external sources to determine right and wrong. Our parents urge us to follow a particular career path expressing their own mistakes and regrets upon us. We listen to our partner who expresses their own insecurities onto us. Our teachers and our coaches inform you, if you want to be the best, it must be done this way.

The key to transforming ourselves and our game into a state of inner confidence is to stop fixating on the rewards that the game may bring, to stop caring about what other people think of our game, but instead to look inward.

This is the difference between grasping at an illusion, the pipe dream and immersing yourself in cultivating your craft. Reality will ground you, liberate, and transform you.

The unauthentic version of you, your false self, is the accumulation of all the external influences in your life which you have internalised and held to be true.

Eventually, you become a stranger to yourself. Your coach is telling you to swing like this, yet you want to emulate certain positions of Rory and Tiger's swing. Confused by a mash of external voices pushing and pulling you to be, do, and act in certain ways. You start to lose confidence in your own ability, you become confused and reliant on others to give you the answers and security which you are now looking for.

Returning to those inclinations and qualities which made you unique, and seeing yourself with a little distance, will help you get out of your head. It will help you to find the way back to playing the game you were meant to play, in your own way. Detachment is a natural ego antidote.

When you start to look inward, you are sparked by what is real to you. Your own way of playing the game. From a certain shot, the way you read a put, to how you visualize tee shots; do you calculate your way around like a mathematician, crunching numbers and making decisions, or do you rely completely on feel and intuition? You let these ideas surface and see what excites you. Sensing these new possibilities and ways of approaching the game, you make a conscious effort to embrace this new way and let go of the way that has not served you.

Reflect back to these memories, dig deep to reveal those childlike intense curiosities within you.

When such reflections have surfaced you determine a direction for your game to take, playing on and off the course. You test, listen closely and explore your internal radar.

Playing analytically on the left side of the brain doesn't work for me. Swing thoughts do the same thing. Taking a single swing thought to the course is setting me up for an anxious, analytically day on the course. I feel stuck and will play from a place of fear which guides the ball around the course. I know this about my own game by turning up to practice and playing in tournaments with just those thoughts.

I would go through months and even years at a time of self-sabotage not listening to my own inclinations for who I am and how I like to play. Instead, I would consume, imitate, and listen to more and more external information. Coaches step in and inform me I should play this way, they would record my swing and compare it to Adam Scott and inform me I needed to be more like him.

My earliest childhood memories are outside in nature. Drawing, writing, building, making things with my hands. From tree houses to bows and arrows, I used my hands and creative mind. I hated things like puzzles, lego, and reading. I remember always seeing and experiencing things in great vivid colors, lines, shapes, and patterns. From this, I can draw some ideas of how to be my authentic self on the golf course.

I see it, feel it, and draw shots in my mind. I feel the rhythm in my body and swing. More importantly, it is important not to practice and slip into bad habits of who I am not. It is this consistent effort to look and seek the answers within, to discover our authentic swing and selves, rather than relying on external stimulus.

When caddying at Claremont Country Club. I could identify members from several hundred yards away by their swing. But when caddying for them they were not tapping into their higher power. They were imitating, they were playing to impress, they were playing from fear. They were playing from ego. When they hit a pure shot, they got out of our own way. Their ego and mind were left at the door.

Our job is to dig deep and find our game within. Figure out who we are and bring that to the table. Playing your game is far more fun than installing other people's beliefs and habits.

Playing like our inner child is peeling back all the layers and connecting to ourselves.

We all want the short cuts and straight path lines to success, but taking the wrong turns, discovering these mistakes is the slow longward journey to you figuring out deep knowledge and insights of your game. These mistakes make you aware of your flaws and toughen you up in the long run. It is perfectly okay to get lost, we all do. Listen closely to the little signs and intricacies that pop up along your journey with the game. We must listen very closely to these queues.

You are now internally driven, rather than motivated or influenced by your external influences and ego. You feel more connected to what you are doing because it is coming from a place that is entirely you and a path that resonates with all your being. Practice now feels exciting and free. You do not feel like you are clock watching, you can focus and play for longer periods of time. You are excited about the learning process of getting better, increasing your skill level, and taking your game to the next level.

You thrive on what many consider "grunt work." you lean into difficult practice as you know this is where the greatest rewards come from. Ten thousand hours to mastery? It doesn't matter. There is no end.

Going about your business in such a way you are thoroughly prepared from within. You feel at one with the game, instead of obsessing over what has happened or what could have been. Opportunities will start to present themself. A putt to break par. A chance to win the Saturday medal.

By finding your own unique way to develop your skills, you will transform your game. We must dream and think big, but act and live small to accomplish what we seek on the fairways. Ambition is part of our being. When we get that light of ambition within us, we must act upon it and embrace our unique calling. Start with the deceptively small things and do them remarkably well.

We all have the chance to be our authentic self and swing our own authentic swing. We get anxious when we are not true to ourselves. We underperform when we are not operating from our authenticity and power.

This process involves a life journey of self-discovery that may even be spiritual. The key to pursuing mastery is to embrace an organic long-term learning process. At the end of this process, we hope to break free from the shackles of the need to prove ourselves. You are enough, you always have been. Only then, the golfer is free.

BONUS 1:

FOR THE GOLFING NERDS - THE FAVORITE GOLFING LIST

Cinderella story. Outta nowhere. A former greenskeeper, now, about to become the Masters champion. It looks like a mirac...It's in the hole! It's in the hole! It's in the hole!

—CARL SPACKLER, CADDYSHACK

- Favourite course: The Berkshire Golf Club, UK
- Favourite clubs of all-time: Mizuno Tp 11, 1990
- Favourite clubs set of all-time: Titleist 975J driver, Taylormade V-Steel 15 degree, 3- LW Mizuno tp 11, Scotty Cameron Tel3
- What's in the bag ATM: Taylormade TP 2008 Driver 8.5 degree, Rocketballz 3 wood 14.5 degree, Callaway Apex Hybrid 22 degree, PXG 0311T 3-6 Iron, Miura CB01 7-PW, Vokey Wedges 52, 56, and 60, 1990 Ping Zing Putter. Ball: Titleist Prov 1
- Superstition: Always align the ball with the number to the right of the Titleist.
- Best golf drill for putting? The Pure Roll
- Best golf drill for wedge game? Lesson no.15
- Best golfing movie? Happy Gilmore, CaddyShack, The legend of Bagger de Vance, Tin Cup. In that order.

- Best swing: Tiger Woods 2008
- Favorite Golfer: Come on....
- Favorite golfing experience: The Halford Hewitt (2 Courses. 64 Schools, 10 players in each team, roughly 640 golfers in total, battle it out at Royal Cinque Ports Golf Club and Royal St George's Golf Club in foursomes until there is a winner.)
- Favourite length of shot? Anything from 125 and in
- Least favourite shot: Big draw with the driver
- Hardest course ever played: PGA National, USA (terrifying)
- Favorite golf books: Inner Game of Tennis, Auto Biography of Bernard Langer, Anything that Bob Rotela Writes
- Dream four ball: Tiger, Rory, Jack
- What would you serve at The Master's Dinner? Starters: Calamari, Mains: Steak, Pudding: Carrot Cake
- Major you would want to win: Tough - but my measurements are 36R
- Best purchase for under £100 to improve your game? Tour Rotation Stick

BONUS 2:

THE MOST RECOMMENDED BOOKS, DRILLS, AND TRAINING AIDS FROM THE PODCAST

When a defining moment comes along, you define the moment, or the moment defines you.

—TIN CUP

Top Most Popular Interviews on the Podcast, "Making A Club Champion"

1. Ep 12: Dave Alred – The Pressure Principles
2. Ep 13: Phil Kenyon – The Putting Principles
3. Ep 26: Adam Young: The Practice Manual: The Ultimate Guide for Golfers
4. Ep 35: Jayne Storey – How to Play your Best Golf through Meditation, Breathing and Quieting the Mind
5. Ep 11: David Galbraith – How to Develop Habits for Success (Psychologist to the All Blacks Rugby 7s Team)
6. Ep 31: Pia Nilsson – How To Birdie Every Hole
7. Ep 27: Sam Jarman – Understanding Happiness On and Off the Golf Course

Most Recommended Books from the Podcast

Focus on 'just-in-time' information instead of 'just-in-case' information."
What part of your game do you need to work on right now? What can
wait for later?

- Inner Game of Golf by Timothy Gallwey
- Golf Is Not A Game of Perfect by Dr Bob Rotella
- Zen Golf by Joseph Parent
- Every shot counts by Mark Broadie
- Bounce by Matthew Syed
- The Chimp Paradox by Steve Peters
- Mastery by Robert Greene
- Ego is the Enemy by Ryan Holiday
- Fearless Golf by Dr Gio Valiante
- Chimp Paradox Model by Steve Peters
- Golf's Sacred Journey by David L. Cook
- My Life In and Out of the Rough by John Daly
- No Limits by Ian Poulter
- Out of the Rough by Steve Williams
- Power of Now by Eckhart Tolle
- Breathe Golf by Jayne Storey
- I Am Pilgrim by Terry Hayes
- Golf the Mind Factor by Darren Clarke and Dr. Karl Morris
- The Pressure Principle by Dave Alred
- If poem by Rudyard Kipling
- Meditations by Marcus Aurelius
- The Talent Code by Daniel Coyle

Most Recommended Training Aids

Why don't you just go HOME? That's your HOME! Are you too good for your HOME? ANSWER ME!

—HAPPY GILMORE

- Putting tutor
- DST Club
- Visio Putting Gates
- Visio Putting Matt
- Putting Mirror
- Swing Plane Factor

Recommended Golf Tech Applications to Improve your Game

- Golf Stat Lab
- 15th Club
- Shots To Hole
- Golf Data Lab
- Golfshot
- Quiet Eye technique
- Focus Band
- 3D Motion Capture System
- Launch Monitor
- TrackMan

Fitness Training Aids

- Mio-Fascia Release Ball
- Rumble Roller

- Yoga Ball
- Theraband
- Pulse Roll
- Stretching Bands
- Balance Pads

Recommended Non/Golf Game Improvers

- Headspace Meditation App
- Calm Meditation App
- The Five Minute Journal

THE BEST 18 MINI TIPS FOR YOUR GAME

I hit a little white ball around a field sometimes.
—RORY MCILROY

Golf is a game that is played on a five-inch course
—BOBBY JONES

These are the best one-liners from golfers I have played with all around the world, who have shared great golfing wisdom and game improver insights.

1. "When you get a great score going, you must stay aggressive and on the attack. Respect the course, but understand you are playing great and keep attacking the course. Now is not the time to get defensive."
2. "If another player wants to hit his putt before you out of turn, let him. This only gives you more time to study your putt."
3. "You can learn more from a putt under a hole than you can above it."
4. Superstitions work for your game if they are positive. Bias is definitely one of our most common traits. When we believe in something, we look for evidence that supports it and dismisses anything that doesn't.

5. "When coming down the stretch with a good score, learn to love the feeling of pressure, absorb all of it, get comfortable with it, this is why you play golf. The feeling of the pump and hitting shots when it matters."

6. "In a head-to-head/match play format and an opponent with a weaker game has got off to a flying start, you have been slow out of the blocks, stay with him right to the end. Keep hitting consistent shots. When it comes down to the back nine and the pressure is on, they can buckle and if you can take them down to the last few holes, you have every chance of winning."

7. "A driver off the deck is your 15th club in the bag, your mind is the 16th."

8. "When playing a chip shot around the green, if you have green to work with, get the ball running early on and use the green. 9/10 you will be more consistent than flying it all the way there."

9. "When hitting putts from off the green, it is a red flag that you have not addressed in your wedge game."

10. "Making a birdie can be a turn in momentum for your round. Be very aware of not giving it back to the course with a bogey the next hole."

11. "Put three balls into your gloves after your round to conserve the lifetime of your glove."

12. "If bored of your clubs, or seeking a change - change the grips, far cheaper, and always feels like a brand-new set every time you play."

13. "In wet weather, put your glove inside the umbrella when walking down the fairway."

14. "Hit right to the left putts out of the toe, straight putts out of the middle, left to the right putts out of the heel." Dave Pelz

15. "Create an email thread with yourself, of all the swing thoughts and feelings you experience that day. Email yourself the ideas that work for you and more importantly which do not."
16. "When practicing, always finish on quality practice. If you practice quality, you are deepening the muscle of quality. Finishing your practice with sloppy and unfocused actions, your mind will internalize that poor form until the next time you show up to practice."
17. "If plugged in the bunker, address the ball on the heel and swing hard"
18. "When traveling abroad with your clubs, flip your clubs the other way round and put the heads at the bottom of your bag, will protect heads from any dinks and dents."

LESSON 19

For all of the most important things, the timing always sucks. Waiting for a good time to quit your job? The stars will never align and the traffic lights of life will never all be green at the same time. The universe doesn't conspire against you, but it doesn't go out of its way to line up the pins either. Conditions are never perfect. "Someday" is a disease that will take your dreams to the grave with you. Pro and con lists are just as bad. If it's important to you and you want to do it "eventually," just do it and correct course along the way.

—TIM FERRISS

How does a writer find his voice? The same way he finds his swing.

—STEVEN PRESSFIELD

One of the most impactful people who I have been fortunate enough to meet during my golfing travels is Mark Bull.

Mark provides 3D analysis and biomechanics services for over 20 leading tour professionals. One English summer day, I spent the afternoon with Mark and my player, who he was coaching, and I was caddying for at the time.

After an inspiring interaction watching both player and coach work things out, I asked Mark for some parting advice on his favorite books in and around golf, psychology, and performance.

"We are all case studies of one. Go write your own book, become your own story, and write it yourself. Why become someone else's value? Get very good at being you again. Be as authentic, be as organic, be a pain, but in a very friendly, pleasant, and enjoyable way. Ask a thousand questions and be the best at being you. "

So, to leave you on that note.

What are, *your* 18 Golfing Secrets?

THE GOLF PERFORMANCE JOURNALS

In 2017 after coming back from caddying on the European Tour, I put together the Golf Data, Long Game, Short Game, Score Better golf performance journals.

Speaking to all the players on tour and asking them about their routines and rituals with the game, their main advice was, "Record, analyze, and measure how you spend your time practicing."

These journals cover each element of your game. The journals are simple. The drills provide you with the room to make it more challenging and measure your performance.

Here is a breakdown of what each book will offer you.

Keep them in your shag bag or travel with them to tournaments.

Score Better Golf Journal: Track, Analyze and Improve Your Game

This book will teach you:

- How to identify your big misses
- How to calculate your shot dispersion
- How to eliminate your most common mistakes
- How to play to your strengths through numbers
- How to identify your weaknesses and optimize your practice time

Golf Data: Performance Statistics About Your Game
This book will teach you...

- How to keep a record of all your tournament and practice rounds
- How to analyze how many fairways, greens, putts, you take during your round
- How to track what side of the course you keep hitting your drives
- How to identify your common misses with all your approach shots

Long Game: 290 yards and In, Driving Range Journal
This book will teach you...

- How to make your range time more effective
- How to implement pressure and real-life tournament conditions
- How to increase your focus through accountability
- How to eliminate one side of the course

Short Game: 125 yards and In. Master Your Wedge Game
This book will teach you...

- How to master your wedge game through yardage systems like Luke Donald
- How to identify your common misses with all your approach shots within 125 yards
- How to "gamify" your short game sessions against the world's best
- How to implement, "go to" shots you can rely on in tournament conditions

Each book will give you the creativity to explore your own unique way of playing the game. It doesn't take much to become impressive when you have a solid structure behind the time invested.

There is always a gap between where you are and where you want to be. Bridging that gap requires just two things: consistent action and consistent focus.

They are all available on Amazon UK, USA, European markets

For USA Global Amazon purchases: The Golf Performance Journals

For UK Amazon purchases: The Golf Performance Journals

IT'S TIME FOR YOU TO SEE THE FIELD

"Look at his practice swing
Almost like he searching for something
And then he finds it
Watch how he settles himself, right into the middle of it
Feel that focus
He got a lot of shots he can choose from
Dufs and tops and skulls
But there is only one shot that's in perfect harmony with the field
One shot that is his, authentic shot
And that shot is going to choose him
There is a perfect shot trying to find each and everyone one of us
And all we got to do is get ourselves out of its way
Let it choose us
Look at him
He can't see that flag as some dragon you got to slay
You got to look with soft eyes
See the place where the tides and the seasons and the turning of the earth
All come together
Where everything that is, becomes one.
You got to seek that place with your soul
Seek it with you hands, don't think about it, feel it
Your hands are wiser than your head will ever going to be.
I can't take you there
Just hope I can help you find a way

It's just you that ball. That flag
And all you are
Seek it with your hands, don't think about it. Feel it
Own your authentic swing
That flag and all that you are.
Welcome to the field." *Bagger Vance*

REVIEWS

I hope you found value from this book.

I would love to know what you think.

If you can leave a review on Amazon, I would be very grateful.

Kia kaha,
Chris

Printed in Poland
by Amazon Fulfillment
Poland Sp. z o.o., Wrocław
23 December 2021

bf822ff6-54fc-4d3c-9438-597b4193a11bR01